EAST ANGLIAN SHORES

EAST ANGLIAN SHORES

David Fairhall

Illustrated by Chris Springham

Published by Adlard Coles Nautical
an imprint of Bloomsbury Publishing Plc
50 Bedford Square, London WC1B 3DP
www.adlardcoles.com

First published by Nautical Books 1988
This edition published by Adlard Coles Nautical 2013

Print ISBN 978-1-4729-0340-2
ePub ISBN 978-1-4729-0341-9
ePDF ISBN 978-1-4729-0342-6

A CIP catalogue record for this book is available from the British Library.

This book is produced using paper that is made from wood grown in managed,
sustainable forests. It is natural, renewable and recyclable. The logging and
manufacturing processes conform to the environmental regulations of the
country of origin.

Typeset by MPS Limited

Note: while all reasonable care has been taken in the publication of this book,
the publisher takes no responsibility for the use of the methods or products
described in the book.

For my children and grandchildren

CONTENTS

CONTENTS

PREFACE

THIS GUIDE IS intended for anyone whose impulse on arriving in an unfamiliar town that has a harbour, river or seashore, is to head for the water. Although I hope it may prove a useful companion to the yachtsman's pilot book, it should sit equally well alongside the motorist's touring map.

The general assumption is that the reader is approaching wherever it may be from the landward side, either by road or rail, probably with an Ordnance Survey map. But he or she may well equally have stepped ashore from a boat, which is how I saw many of these harbours and quaysides for the first time.

Chris Springham and I worked systematically north from the Thames to the Wash, from Leigh to Lynn, touching at almost every place where one can get access to the water. We have assumed that others – including those who have crossed the North Sea – share our curiosity as to how the East Anglian coast came to look as it does today, why the harbours were built there, and by whom. What sort of craft use them? What fish do they catch from those boats drawn up on the beach? Is there anything special about the church on the hill? Where can you take a walk without being accused of trespassing? Are there any decent pubs or restaurants? Any buildings or museums worth searching out, especially on a rainy day?

Although the book is obviously written primarily for an English readership, I hope it may also prove useful for Dutch visitors to East Anglia – of whom there are many, particularly yachtsmen. In working round the coastline I have found innumerable references to Dutch influence, to joint ventures, rivalry, and sometimes of course enmity – as when Admiral de Ruyter tried to take Harwich. We even share a maritime language, in words like pier, hard, sluice or yacht.

Finally, let me admit to an enthusiastic bias in my writing: a tendency to assume that this corner of England is God's own country.

David Fairhall

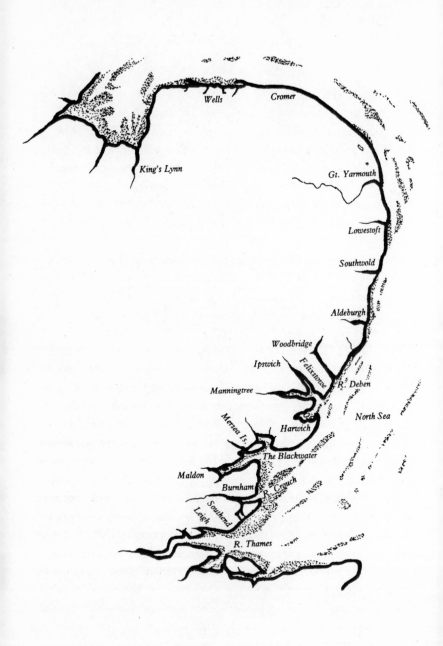

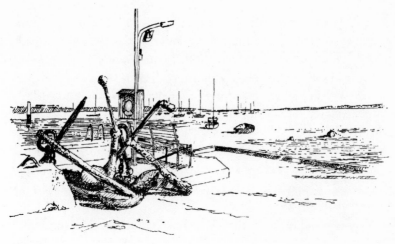

Orford Quay.

INTRODUCTION

> Then up reared a conger as long as a mile;
> 'Wind's comin' easterly', he says with a smile.

THESE SINISTER LINES, from an old song the sailing barge skipper Bob Roberts used to sing, convey something simple but fundamental about this coast: its particular perspective on the weather.

The westerly gales that drive ships onto the rocky shores of Cornwall or Scotland bring fewer problems to this corner of Britain; it is the east wind which turns it into an exposed lee shore. And whereas in summer an easterly breeze is often associated with fine, dry weather, in winter that same wind feels as if it has come all the way from the Arctic – as indeed it probably has – driving flocks of migrating birds before it and flattening the stunted marshland trees.

It has been said of the Essex marshlands in particular that they seem 'set to the key of winter'; but even in winter, the region's wide bright skies tend to lift the spirits rather than depress them. The sort of depression that worries people round here is the meteorological variety that brings a storm surge funnelling down the North Sea just when an exceptionally high spring tide is also expected. That is what happened on the night of 31 January, 1953 when many people drowned in the cold flood water. Since then the Thames Barrier has been built to protect central London, and earthen sea walls all round the coasts of Essex, Suffolk and Norfolk have been raised to at least the 1953 peak tide level.

These floods are part of the folk memory of East Anglia. I remember my own astonishment at seeing miles of water where there used to be fields; trees were shrivelled by salt far inland, on streams one never thought could be connected with the sea.

In many places you will find the 1953 flood level recorded: on a brick wall, on the side of a waterside pub, and in King's Lynn on the church porch. It illustrates what I suspect is a regional characteristic – a sense of history. People in these coastal communities tend to be conscious of their ancestry, of how the local fisheries have changed, of the date on which erosion finally sent the old church toppling over the cliff, or where the Vikings are believed to have landed for a bout of rape and pillage. As in Ireland, there is a tendency to talk about the past as if it were part of the present.

It is sometimes said of the East Anglian communities that they are wary of strangers, rather introverted in their loyalties. But then much of the coastal region remains surprisingly remote, especially since the railway closures of the 1960s. Road links too are relatively poor – though good enough to have wiped out most of the coastwise shipping that used to serve mills, farms, factories and power stations across innumerable small wharves.

Any tour of East Anglian harbours is therefore inclined to become an exercise in nostalgia. Yet there are striking exceptions, such as the explosive growth of Felixstowe's modern container port, or the vigorous way Great Yarmouth has adapted itself to cater for the new oil, gas and wind farm industries.

Nor have the traditional fisheries necessarily disappeared, though the North Sea herring stocks are virtually destroyed and Continental beam trawlers play havoc with the flatfish. Most of the harbours between Leigh to Lynn still shelter a small, albeit dwindling fleet of boats. Many of them are part-timers, it is true, but the local catches are the same as ever: oysters, sprats, cockles and mussels, shrimps, whelks, sole, cod, plaice, dabs, skate (or roker, as they call it on this coast); even the occasional 'shimmer' of herring. A few bold spirits experiment with new fishing methods and venture further afield, as they always did. Several fisheries are once more expanding.

In navigational terms the Thames Estuary does not end at Southend Pier; it fills the whole triangle of sea between Lowestoft and the North Foreland of Kent. Not until a ship is fifteen or twenty miles offshore does it get clear of the drying sandbanks into permanently deep water. These banks have ancient, evocative names: Gunfleet, Shipwash, Buxey, Barrow, Sunk. At sea they are marked by lonely beacons with sandy green North Sea water swirling past their iron legs. It scours mainly from southwest to northeast in the direction of the ebb tide. Few channels run across the basic tidal stream, usually just shallow swatchways where even the navigator of a small yacht keeps an eye on the depth sounder.

Off Suffolk and Norfolk the sands become fewer, although those that remain – Corton, Scroby, Haisboro' – have formidable reputations. Some of the first lifeboats were established along this shore, and with good reason. Few of the small harbours are safely accessible in strong onshore winds.

Finally, beyond Hunstanton, the Wash opens up with another broad swathe of banks and channels, one of which leads into the Great Ouse for King's Lynn.

This coast's two predominant habitats are marshland, fringed with black glutinous mud, and shingle beaches backed by sandy cliffs, dunes and heath.

To the uninitiated, black mud must sound less than inviting. But as a setting for the ebb and flow of the tide it has its own esoteric beauty. It's only black when you disturb it; the surface is normally covered with a grey sheen. And for some reason it does not *feel* dirty. The kids love wallowing in it anyway, and at Maldon even the adults hurl themselves into the annual mud race, finishing black and exhausted on the quayside outside the Queen's Head.

The mud also attracts wading birds in their thousands, with long articulated legs and probing beaks. And especially, as every radio and television producer knows, the wintering curlew. Its wild cry has become the signature tune of the marshes, just as the raucous, echoing call of the herring gull suggests a setting somewhere on the rocky western coasts.

Between sea wall and mudflats there is generally a stretch of green saltings – stiffer mud bound together by specialised salt water plants like the sea pink and the sea lavender, which dust the green with a delicate mauve blush each summer. Samphire, a succulent plant growing in the soft edges of the saltings, is a traditional marshland delicacy, eaten boiled like asparagus. It's an equivalent of the sea kale and sea pea one finds on the beaches of Suffolk or Norfolk. But the mud offers nothing quite so special as the sea holly, trembling on the shingle in an onshore breeze, nor anything so spectacular as the yellow horned poppy.

Moving north from Essex into Suffolk and Norfolk, broad muddy estuaries give way to narrower rivers, still muddy inside but choked at their seaward end by sandy bars. The north Norfolk coast is different again: great shingle banks penetrated by the sea every few miles to provide a precarious haven, scoured clean and dry by fierce tides. Both these counties offer great bird-watching country: a chance to see avocets, harriers, and Broadland's bitterns and bearded tits.

The East Anglian coastline has evolved an astonishing variety of commercial sailing craft, some of which survive as yachts; a few still earn their living powered by diesel engines instead of canvas. Towering above them all, both physically and metaphorically, is the Thames spritsail barge – a flat-bottomed 150-tonner that can be handled by two men and is equally at home smashing her way through the short waves of the North Sea or gliding up some half-tide creek. A miracle of versatility, and beautiful with it.

The Thames also produced a sort of cousin to the sailing barge, the bawley, a fishing vessel that can now only be seen preserved as a yacht, though the shallow-draft cocklers that developed alongside it still work out of Leigh Creek. The Colne and Blackwater built elegant, yacht-like smacks, many of which are still enthusiastically sailed and raced. The bawley is also associated with Harwich, and then gives way to the beach boats of Suffolk and Norfolk.

The magnificent beach yawls have gone completely. Indeed one wonders how anyone ever ventured to sail them off an exposed shore: open boats up to 70 feet long, driven so fast by their powerful lugsails they could hold the lee gunwhale under without taking water aboard. But small, plump, transom-sterned fishing boats still launch off the steep shingle at Aldeburgh and elsewhere. Cromer still has its small fleet of crabbers, though only one of the traditional wooden double-enders is now working.

The great fleets of Lowestoft sailing trawlers and drifters rapidly disappeared as steam power took hold. And the Broadland wherry, a humbler, black-sailed equivalent of the Thames barge, was close to extinction when the Norfolk Wherry Trust stepped in to preserve the *Albion*.

A procession of white Bermudan-rigged yachts is no substitute for this rich historical pattern. But in terms of hull form and cargo handling, the commercial craft continue to evolve and adapt in the same way they always did. Some rapidly specialise, like Yarmouth's offshore supply vessels, developed to serve the North Sea gas and oil industries. In evolutionary terms you could describe them as a branch of the tug family, with a towering great superstructure forward, trailing behind it a flat, uncluttered working platform as close to the water as any tug or barge, and able to manoeuvre in under the rigs. The offshore wind farms are serviced by specialised catamarans. Other vessels retain a deliberate versatility, so as to poke their bows wherever there is the chance of a profitable cargo.

Between Leigh and Lynn you will find all the main types at work: deep-laden tankers, nippy little roll-on roll-off ferries, vast slab-sided container ships, rusty suction dredgers, bulkers in the grain trade, stocky square-sterned trawlers, and passenger ferries whose piled-up decks bear less and less resemblance to the traditional graceful form of a seagoing ship. In many cases new ships and new trades have been slotted into existing ports with only minimal reconstruction ashore. Elsewhere, notably at Felixstowe where a completely new port has grown like a cuckoo in the Harwich nest, the whole infrastructure has been rebuilt.

Yet this coast is still predominantly rural. Many of its havens have not changed their basic character over hundreds of years. Though irreversible silting and the increasing size of ships may have reduced their relative importance, their history is continuous and alive. A few small riverside wharves still work 'grain out and timber in'.

Physically, the coastline has slowly been smoothed and rounded by a combination of reclamation and erosion. Man-made sea walls have closed tidal gaps. Various promontories or 'nesses' have spread shingle southwards to block an adjacent estuary. Shipden Ness, which used to project from the Norfolk coast near Cromer, has disappeared altogether. So has the medieval town of Dunwich, which once stood on the low, crumbling cliffs between Aldeburgh and Southwold.

Ashore, the East Anglian landscape is flat and open to the sky. Look at the illustrations in this book: most are naturally horizontal. Any vertical line, whether it be a ship's mast, a lighthouse, a church tower or a refinery flare stack, makes a disproportionate impact. Otherwise the scene is likely to be filled with great swathes of sea, sand, cornfields and clouds.

How far this explains why so many of our great landscape painters should have worked in this area, I leave you to judge. The 18th century painter Crome, founder of the Norwich School, obviously thought it was directly important. Asked by his son why he had chosen Mousehold

Heath as the subect of the painting now in the National Gallery, he said 'for air and space'. Gainsborough was another local man, born in Sudbury and married in Ipswich. And then of course there is Constable, whose work has made the Stour valley a place of tourist pilgrimage.

Low tide at Leigh Creek.

1

THE THAMES, HAVENGORE
AND THE ROACH

LEIGH – HADLEIGH – SOUTHEND – SHOEBURY – PAGLESHAM

THERE ARE SEVERAL excellent reasons for starting a guide to the East Anglian harbours at Leigh, in Essex. It's a pretty little place, full of the scruffy, unpretentious charm that distinguishes much of this easterly shore from the smoother, more cultivated harbours of the South Coast – and the only place I know where you can find a beach made entirely of cockle shells.

It is also the last harbour on the north bank of the Thames – though admittedly not much of a refuge unless a boat takes the ground comfortably at low tide – before the river opens out into a great fan-shaped estuary of sandbanks stretching from there to Lowestoft. Ships and men have migrated back and forth along these channels in search of fish, trade or just deeper water. To take one example: the new technique of cockle dredging originally tried out at Leigh in the 1960s rapidly spread as far as King's Lynn on the Wash.

Cockling apart, the type of fishing vessel traditionally associated with Leigh is the sailing bawley. It was Leigh's contribution to our maritime heritage; a broad-beamed beauty that to my eye is more attractive than its superficially more elegant sisters on the Colne.

But before taking a close look at the cockle boat and the bawley, one needs to put Leigh into some sort of geographical perspective. And the best way of doing that if you approach along the A13, the old London road before they built the Southend arterial, is to turn off at Hadleigh and view the estuary from its ruined castle, now an official historical monument.

For obvious military reasons the castle was built on a high grassy bluff commanding the shallow glacial valley of the Thames. Long since ruined but with a couple of towers still standing, it was the product of 13th century power politics. Hubert de Burgh, Earl of Kent, owned the land in those days and a lot of his building material was Kentish ragstone. But before he could finish the job he was disgraced at Court; the buildings fell into royal hands and remained there until 1551.

By the time John Constable turned up in 1814 to make a pencil sketch for his painting of the castle (another, painted sketch can be seen in the Tate Gallery) it had already been derelict for two centuries. 'I walked upon the beach at South End', he told his future wife Maria Bicknell. 'I was always delighted with the melancholy grandeur of a seashore. At Hadleigh there is a ruin of a castle which from its situation is a really fine place – it commands a view of the Kent hills, the Nore and North Foreland and looking many miles to sea.' It's still a fine place. Much of what Constable saw remains, though sighting the North Foreland from that distance must always have been rather ambitious. But the western skyline is now punctuated by the refinery flare stacks of Coryton and the rest – more reminiscent of Lowry.

Since the construction of the new London Gateway container port, the 400 or so ships which pass here every week will increasingly include vast creatures each stacked with many thousands of cargo containers. With a draft of up to perhaps 50ft or more, and a nearly square-sectioned hull 'sniffing' the bottom as they work their way through the sands, these leviathans will have begun their approach at the Sunk, 10 miles off Harwich; then down the Black Deep channel, past the tide gauge on the Shivering Sand Tower (characteristic names, which evoke the melancholy Constable noticed in this estuary), closely monitored on the radar displays of the Vessel Traffic Service at Gravesend.

Immediately below the castle, on the far side of Hadleigh Ray, is Canvey Island. Its eastern end is covered with a dreary bungaloid development, yet for yachtsmen, or at least for the multihull enthusiasts, this ought to be some sort of shrine. It was here in the early 1950s, working from a converted garage on Smallgains Creek, that the Prout brothers developed the ancient Pacific catamaran into a modern yacht.

Roland and Francis Prout were highly successful racing canoeists who had competed in the Helsinki Olympics. They read about the outrigger canoes and catamarans sailed by the Pacific islanders, and conceived the idea of lashing two of their moulded ply canoes together with a lightweight bamboo structure and setting a National 12 dinghy mainsail on top. It worked. The next step was to produce a purpose-built 17-foot version they called the Shearwater. That worked even better, and at Burnham it cleaned up in the D Class handicap.

The racing committee were alarmed by this strange craft's extraordinary turn of speed; it was not a proper boat, they decided. But the Prouts persevered, and received a big boost when the Royal Burnham Yacht Club adopted the Shearwater as a class. More than two thousand were eventually built, and catamarans rapidly evolved into cruising boats as well as racers.

Canvey has another story to tell from the early 1950s. In the great flood of 1953 (and you will find that along this coast almost everyone who is old enough remembers it vividly) Canvey Island was among the hardest hit. Many elderly people lived there in chalets and bungalows. Behind its sea walls, the whole island lies below the level even of ordinary spring tides, and on that occasion the walls were suddenly breached by a freak storm surge in the cold darkness of a winter's night.

Looking east from Hadleigh, Leigh Creek lies between you and the grey line of Southend Pier. At high tide the creek is lost in an uninterrupted stretch of water scattered with small craft. At low tide you may be able to follow the line of the narrow gutway winding out towards deep water, the boats now lying at awkward angles on its muddy banks – a situation that explains why Southend's lifeboat station operates a small hovercraft alongside its conventional inshore boat.

'Old Leigh', as opposed to Leigh-on-Sea, is squeezed against its creek by the railway line that was driven through the town in 1856. You can park as you drop down over the railway line, or cross by one of the footbridges. In spite of the name, there are few really old buildings. Those that remain have probably been refaced in the soft, yellow, stock bricks that are characteristic of Victorian Essex as well as London. Yet in medieval times Leigh was a major port, comparable with Colchester if not with Harwich. The *Mayflower*, which took the Pilgrims to America in 1620, is supposed to have been built in one of its shipyards, and called there on the way round from Harwich before crossing the Atlantic.

Even when Leigh Creek began to silt up the fishing fleet continued to thrive, augmented in the 19th century as industrialisation polluted the upper reaches of the Thames and steam trains appeared to carry fresh fish back up to Billingsgate. Local boats still go after sole, sprats, whitebait and brown shrimps, as well as cockles. But it was the shrimping that produced the beautiful bawley; the name is simply a corruption of 'boiler boat', a smack that boiled shrimp on board on her way back from the grounds.

One of Leigh's waterside pubs is called The Peter Boat, by association with a smaller type of fishing craft that was once extremely common on the Thames. Perhaps 20 feet long, it was spritsail rigged like the Thames sailing barges, with a clinker built double-ended hull reminiscent of a Norfolk crab boat; they probably shared the same Viking ancestry. It sounds unlikely, but according to the maritime historians it was the peter boat which evolved during the 19th century into the much bigger, broad shouldered, square-sterned bawley. Nowadays you will only see the bawley as a carefully preserved yacht, or roughly cut down to a motor boat, or as just an abandoned hulk on the saltings. At the turn of the last century there were about 80 registered at Leigh, each working up to four shrimp nets at a time. Massive stability enabled them to carry an exceptionally high sailplan based on a boomless gaff mainsail. And it was this tall, dignified silhouette, reminiscent of the sailing barges alongside which many bawleys were built, that made them so attractive.

The distinctive lines and equipment of a Leigh cockler.

But you do not have to be nostalgic to enjoy an outing to Leigh, with old established pubs like The Crooked Billet, an art gallery, a 'heritage centre' and – if you arrive by a suitable boat – a couple of small wharves where you could take the ground. 'Cockle teas' are still available, and at least for some of the older, visiting Londoners, remain a ritual accompaniment to the funfairs of Southend.

The sheds where the cockles are boiled stand at the western end of the waterside. Each shed has one or more cockle boats supplying it: a fleet of ten when I last enquired. You will see them at low tide leaning against the side of the creek, a plank running ashore to a beach heaped high with empty shells. The cockle boat evolved separately from the bawley, with a shallower form to enable it to be run conveniently ashore on the sands while the crew raked and loaded the cockles. And of course it is now driven by a powerful diesel engine. This enables a cockler to speed the raking by dropping an anchor astern in a likely spot and swinging in circles as the tide recedes so as to 'blow' the shellfish into a central heap.

The big change in fishing methods started in the 1960s when the White Fish Authority helped one of the local boats to experiment with a water-pumped dredge instead of the traditional hand raking. Water pumped through the dredge by an auxiliary engine sweeps the cockles up through a large diameter pipe and across a rotating sieve on deck. Instead of having to go out on one tide, dry out on the Maplin sands to rake and load, then return on the next tide, a dredging crew can fill their hold with seven or eight tons of cockles in a few hours. But they still have to wait until the flooding tide fills their home creek before coming in to unload, and it's then that the place really comes alive. Along this coast it usually pays to time a quayside visit for high water if you want to see what makes that particular place tick.

At Leigh one can wander in and out of the quayside buildings, sampling shellfish or beer, until the narrow strip of land beneath the railway runs out altogether at the eastern end. From there a footpath leads along the beach to where a retired naval minesweeper has been run ashore as a clubhouse for the Essex Yacht Club.

This is the home of the Estuary One-Design, an 18-foot racing dinghy class amalgamated from the Essex One-Design, which I believe does not set a spinnaker, and the Thames Estuary One-Design, which does. The E.O.D. is one of several little traditional, bluff-bowed, half-decked one-designs that are still enthusiastically raced from the Essex rivers alongside the newer high-tech boats, and not everywhere in dwindling numbers. All were originally clinker-built in wood, but the E.O.D. has made the transition to fibreglass construction.

From Leigh eastwards, the seafront road runs through the technicolor of Southend to a slightly gloomy dead end at Shoeburyness. In addition to the massed ranks of parked cars, someone has counted more than 3,000 small boat moorings along this exposed, muddy shore.

Straddling it is the 1¼ mile lattice of Southend Pier, boasted to be the longest in the world. It was started in 1830 and extended to more or less its present length 16 years later to reach deep water where cargoes could be unloaded and passengers embarked at any state of the tide. Paddle steamer services eventually linked all the main piers along the East Coast with London. But a structure of that size athwart the stream was bound to be a hazard as well as a convenience: at least 20 biggish vessels have run into it over the years. The concrete schooner *Molliette* which lies wrecked off Mersea Island was one. In 1986 a 600-ton coaster smashed straight through it near the end, marooning a couple of anglers.

Unlikely as it seems, unless you know what lies on the marshes beyond, Shoeburyness is an old established Army garrison town, with street names like Gunners Road. The 'ness' comes from an Old English word you will find all along the East Coast – also spelt 'nass' and 'naze' – to indicate a shingle spit or promontory; it originally meant nose.

Like the shingle 'hards' that are used for boat landings, such features are much appreciated in an area where so much of the shoreline consists of soft black mud. At the same time their tendency to extend across the entrance to harbours as a result of coastal erosion has caused endless trouble.

Skirt round the Shoeburyness barracks and you will come to East Beach. Nothing particularly attractive about it, but a vantage point from which one can look out across the five mile expanse of the Maplin Sands, where in the late 1960s they were planning to build London's third airport. The only visible remainder of that abortive scheme is a small hummock on the skyline where ships turn northeast along the Swin Channel, a trial bank of large shingle laid by reclamation engineers and now visited only by birdwatchers and the occasional curious yachtsman.

The other work begun before the airport project was cancelled was clearing the thousands of shells – the military kind, not the ones containing cockles – that lie buried in these sands. The Maplins, and the Foulness Sand beyond, form a 30,000-acre military firing range.

Lieutenant Colonel Shrapnel (whose name tells you what he invented) turned up here in 1805 and asked permission from the Lord of the Manor to carry out experiments with his new-fangled exploding cannonball. The Army have been at Shoeburyness more or less ever since, and in permanent residence since 1856 – although the ranges are nowadays managed by a commercial company. They are used to develop new types of gun or ammunition and to carry out routine safety checks on existing stocks – and not just for the soldiers. Naval gun turrets have also been tested here, and an expensive carcass of the RAF's cancelled TSR-2 bomber was set up on one of the ranges to discover the effect of various kinds of ammunition on high-performance aircraft structures.

The setting for all this military activity is a network of marshy creeks and islands whose most numerous population consists of black brent geese and flocks of small wading birds. But a few people do live and farm on the main island of Foulness in long-established partnership with the soldiers. It's a strange, private little world which outsiders can normally penetrate only if they have some business on the islands, such as visiting one of the residents. Two exceptions to the rule are the road to Wakering Stairs, which is open to the public when firing is not in progress, and Havengore Creek, through which fishermen and yachtsmen retain the right of passage by arrangement with the Army.

Wakering Stairs are important as the starting point of what is known as the Broomway, an ancient road across the sands which can still be traced at low tide, and which linked the islands before the muddy creeks were dammed or bridged. They say it's the only place where a sailing barge has been known to collide with a coal cart – from which the horse had hurriedly been unhitched. It's certainly a dangerous place for men or horses to be caught out on a rising tide because the sea floods suddenly across miles of almost totally flat sands. That is what attracted the gunners; they can test fire shells into the water at high tide and then recover them for inspection as soon as the water drains away. And this is also where the Leigh cocklers find their shellfish.

As the name suggests, Havengore was once a harbour in its own right. That was in the days when the main deep water route running north from the River Crouch also ran inshore along what is now no more than a shallow swatchway called the Ray Sand. The Havengore entrance is now a narrow gutway accessible to shoal-draft boats only on the top of the tide. The Essex Yacht Club's E.O.D.s traditionally use it on their way round to race in Burnham Week, and enthusiastic 'ditch crawlers' among the East Coast yachtsmen occasionally like to exercise their right of navigation just as keen ramblers maintain public rights of way along ancient footpaths.

Havengore Creek is spanned by a lifting bridge which is raised at request for fishing boats and yachts to pass through. Inside the constricted entrance a network of steep-sided mud channels leads through to the deep water of the River Roach, which in turn joins the River Crouch near its mouth. In spite of the sound of gunfire – or rather because of it – these are some of the most peaceful, secluded creeks on the East Coast. But of course the trade-off is their inaccessibility except by water. At the turn of the century they were frequented by sailing barges, the Wakering 'brickies' that raced one another across the Maplins to be first to load at the brickfields just inside the entrance.

Until a few years ago, an occasional coaster would penetrate the final mud-filled tentacle of the Roach to serve the old mills at Stambridge, near Rochford. But nowadays most of the activity is among the fishing boats moored at a spot known locally as The Violet, between Potton Island and Barling Ness. This is the creek you see on your right hand if you look across from the other side of the Roach, at Paglesham Eastend.

Paglesham gives public access to the river – but only just. By road, you head east from Rochford across a fine stretch of Essex cornland (Dutch elm disease has destroyed many of the great trees that used to break the skyline). Fork right where the signpost offers a choice between Churchend and Eastend, and when the tarmac peters out you will find the pretty little Plough and Sail pub. This was the scene of an historic confrontation over pints of beer between our former Prime Minister Edward Heath (himself a yachtsman) and the 'Defenders of Essex' – followed not long afterwards, as it happens, by cancellation of the Maplin Airport project (there is of course once again talk of a new London airport in the estuary, but if so, it would be on the other side of the Thames).

Alongside the pub a desperately unmade road leads down to a boatyard car park and the waterside. Beyond the sea wall is Paglesham hard, formerly the haunt of traditionalist East Coast yachtsmen who would sooner hoist their paraffin riding light in some quiet creek than jostle into a marina. The modern yard seems to specialise in motor craft, but an older tradition of barge and smack building is represented by the black weatherboarded shed on the seaward side of the wall. Hervey Benham in *Down Tops'l* tells the story of the barge which launched herself from there one morning. The boatbuilders had manoeuvred her onto the slipway outside the shed and gone home for breakfast. When they returned she was afloat in the river and not even the oyster dredgermen working nearby had seen her go (oysters, by the way, are once again being cultivated in the nearby 'pool').

Paglesham can be worth a visit to exercise pedestrians' right of way along the sea wall, if only to get a feel for that maze of marshy waterways beyond it that is mostly hidden behind barbed wire. Nearby, hidden berneath the saltings, are the remnants of HMS *Beagle*, in which the young Charles Darwin visited the Galapagos islands in 1835. A number of local farmers' barns, it seems, were subsequently constructed from her abandoned timbers.

2

THE CROUCH

CANEWDON – WALLASEA ISLAND – HULLBRIDGE – BATTLESBRIDGE –
FAMBRIDGE – BURNHAM

THE CROUCH IS A fine deep river for racing yachtsmen. It runs
almost due east for 15 miles from Battlesbridge to Shore Ends, with
one of the East Coast's great yachting centres, Burnham-on-Crouch,
midway along its northern bank. But even its most loyal advocates
might admit that the straight uniformity of the lower reaches makes
them rather dull, an acquired taste at least. Beating in against the ebb
can certainly be tedious when you are not racing. The view is blocked by
high sea walls, and indeed that is the place to be, not on the water, if you
want to take in the surrounding countryside.

If it is possible to live on the wrong side of the tracks, then Wallasea
Island, adjacent to Paglesham on the southern bank of the Crouch,
might be said to be on the wrong side of the water. Its main interest
is the Baltic Wharf, where big timber carriers from Russia and
Scandinavia give some scale to the seemingly endless rows of moored

yachts. There is a marina, but nothing so grand as the 'royal' yacht clubs on the other bank.

Yet if one goes back into English history, the royal connections on this side of the Crouch make Burnham opposite seem no more than a 19th century upstart. Take Canewdon. It was from this hill on 18 October, 1016 that the Danish King Canute launched his forces against the Saxon Edmund Ironsides, encamped on Ashingdon Hill just to the west. The Battle of Ashingdon was of far greater strategic, if not literary, significance than the Battle of Maldon 25 years earlier. Canute won, and ruled England for years afterwards.

The site of the battle is pretty well established, between the two hills in the vicinity of Scaldhurst Farm on the river side of the Ashingdon–Canewdon road. Far more speculative is the place where Canute tried to turn back the tide; Cliff Reach just upstream from Burnham is one possibility, but there are dozens of others. Nor, sadly, can one neatly connect Canewdon with the Danish warrior by explaining that it means 'Canute's hill'. I would have been inclined to the journalist's dictum 'Don't confuse me with facts' had I not been disillusioned years ago by Archie White's *Tideways and Byeways*. He refers readers to *The Place-names of Essex* which talks about 'this difficult name' and suggests that it probably means 'the hill of Cana's people'.

One is on rather firmer ground in linking Canewdon with another battle and another king. Above the west door of the church tower are three badly weathered escutcheons, the middle once bearing the arms of King Henry V, with those of his mother's family, the Bohuns, on the right. Henry is believed to have commissioned this massive 85-foot, pale grey ragstone tower as a thanksgiving for his victory at Agincourt in 1415. The tower especially makes this church worth a visit. It dominates the valley from what we flatlanders reckon quite a substantial hill, surrounded in season by golden fields of wheat or barley. Ask permission and you can climb the 102 spiral steps inside the tower to get an even better view from the top. Just outside the churchyard on the other side are the well-preserved 18th century village stocks and lockup.

A check of the Ordnance Survey contours shows that Canewdon hill is little more than 100 feet high. It makes an impact, and the church with it, because it rises from reclaimed salt marshes that are below high tide level, as the 1953 floods demonstrated. Unfortunately the modern bungalow builders in this part of Essex seem to have lost sight of the need for architectural height and dignity, perhaps because land is relatively cheap. Driving along the upper reaches of the Crouch there is precious little attraction except sudden glimpses of the river itself, stretched at the foot of gently sloping fields or discovered at the bottom of some potholed lane with a characteristic jumble of small cruising yachts, motor boats and converted lifeboats.

On the south bank above Canewdon there is public road access to the water at Hullbridge, which has little to recommend it to a casual visitor. But there is a large pub right on the waterside, or rather where the river runs out of water at low tide. It was forded here to reach South Woodham Ferrers.

The road crossing is at Battlesbridge (paradoxically, nothing to do with any ancient battles). The old mill building by the quay and the names of the two pubs, the Barge and the Hawk, recall the time when this was a trading point for the local farms, served by sailing barges and small coasters that could wriggle up on a spring tide. Now most of the buildings have been converted as showrooms for antiques, though some restoration work has been carried out on the old tide mill above the bridge (now containing a shop), so as to generate electricity from a reconstructed water wheel. Until it stopped grinding corn at the turn of the century, it was said to have been the most powerful mill in the area.

Heading back along the north bank of the Crouch, you come first to South Woodham Ferrers; the original village had its own wharf in Clementsgreen Creek. Bricks shipped out by barge helped feed the 19th century expansion of London, but by the turn of the century this was one of the first places to begin absorbing refugees from the overcrowded capital. Here and elsewhere in southeast Essex, land that was no longer worth farming was auctioned off to trainloads of cockneys looking for some escape from the smoke. Hundreds of small plots were sold for £5,

£10 or £20, with the return fare paid and perhaps a glass of champagne for those signing up; indeed they were known as 'champagne sales'. And there were few awkward building regulations to prevent people putting up a simple house and trying to earn a living from their small holding, as many did.

The resulting development became known as the 'plotlands'. At South Woodham Ferrers the migration from London continued, though in a quite different form – an ambitious new town where architects have made a brave attempt to create artificially the varied, higgledy piggledy atmosphere of an old established community.

Next stop along the railway branch line to Southminster is North Fambridge. A lane takes you down to the Ferry Boat Inn, tucked in alongside the boatyard behind post-1953 sea defences. Over on the saltings, with their own neat little sea wall in place of a garden fence, are four archetypal weatherboarded Essex cottages. Mike Peyton, the cartoonist, a local of many years' standing, tells me they were built with drain plugs in the floors, so much was periodic flooding taken for granted. Mike's recommendation for a walk from there is to use the railway for a round trip to Althorne: one stop down the line and three miles back along the sea wall, or the other way round, depending on the wind direction. Downstream, the walk takes you past Bridgemarsh Island which can also be reached by the private unmade road to Althorne's small boatyard.

Bridgemarsh is a case of land reclaimed not from the sea but by the sea. It was once farmed, but if you arrive at high tide you will find only the sea walls standing above water, plus a few brick remnants of the old farm buildings opposite the hard. Story has it that the farmer failed to notice how badly the walls had been undermined by rabbits. In the winter of 1928 a big tide finally overwhelmed them and swept out again, widening the breach and carrying the farm's haystacks with it.

The Southminster line (long may it last) is one of a dwindling number that used to serve the small harbours of the East Coast. Maldon, Tollesbury, Brightlingsea, Aldeburgh, Snape, Southwold, all had their own little branches now useful only as footpaths. Maurice Griffiths, formerly editor of *Yachting Monthly,* wrote affectionately of pre-war days when the Great Eastern Railway made special weekend tickets available to yachtsmen on these 'crab and winkle' services. He could take a train to Maldon on Friday night, sail to, say, Aldeburgh and return to London on the same ticket.

Modern rail operators are not so discriminating, but at Burnham you can still join a yacht by train. And having been rather disparaging about its river, I must say that Burnham itself is a delight, whether you come by rail, road or water. Approaching overland from the west, you follow one of those characteristic Essex country roads (G. K. Chesterton would have approved) that zig-zag along the edge of every field round a series of right-angle bends instead of cutting straight across. You then cross the railway and turn into a broad High Street running the length of the waterfront.

Burnham always seems such a cheerful place. Perhaps it's the visual effect of the warm red and yellow brickwork set off by white painted weatherboarding. The double-width High Street can absorb a few parked cars without fuss. It has never been organised into a formal parade of shops; in fact it looks much as it did in Victorian photographs: a few imposing double-fronted houses mingling with smart little cottages, shops, inns and restaurants. A handsome clock tower erected by public subscription in 1877 in memory of some local dignitary adds a finishing touch.

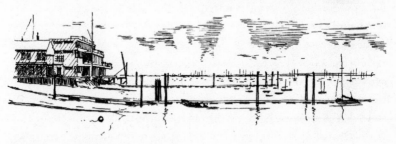

The Royal Corinthian Yacht Club at Burnham.

It's handy for visitors that several pubs, where one can eat as well as drink, look out across the sea wall. The moment you step up there you realise what a vast yachting centre this little riverside town has become. The whole place seems to be devoted to boating in one form or another. Among its prestigious yacht clubs are the Crouch Yacht Club, the Royal Burnham, closely associated with the town, and at the far end of the waterfront the Royal Corinthian, which migrated here from the Thames and later sent an offspring to Cowes. The name Corinthian was chosen in 1872 to indicate that members wanted to do their own sailing in relatively small yachts, not dependent on paid hands.

Among the many classes that race here in Burnham Week, the two 'royal' clubs are especially proud of the small one-designs they both developed in the 1930s and which still survive: the Royal Burnham, a beamy, transomed sterned 20-footer by Norman Dallimore; the Royal Corinthian's a sleeker design by Harry Smith, with a short counter stern. Both classes were severely battered in the great storm of October 1987, but you will see them moored in line immediately off their respective clubs; identical shapes, yet great care taken to choose a distinctive colour scheme.

Not many yacht clubs can boast of their architectural significance. Yet the Royal Corinthian's uncompromising rectangular clubhouse was a radical trendsetter in its day. The architect was Joseph Emberton, who also designed the Empire Hall at Olympia and Simpsons in Piccadilly. His Burnham design looks at first as if it's built in ferroconcrete. In fact he chose a lightweight steel structure filled in with rendered brickwork and supported on piles driven into the river side of the sea wall. Tiers of balconies project over the water, backed by continuous metal framed windows.

The clubhouse was reckoned a great success when it opened in 1931 and it won an RIBA Medal for the architect. Today it looks heavily dated, but opinions will vary as to whether that matters.

In one of his books about sailing barges, Bob Roberts tells of drifting up the Crouch in a November fog and calling to the mate if he could see Burnham yet. No, came the shouted reply, but he had sighted a 'flour mill' on the bank ahead. Emberton would probably have been pleased by that.

Beyond the Royal Corinthian, the sea wall path leads out towards Holliwell Point with the great expanse of the Dengie marshes on the left. If you like a walk with a bit of a challenge to it, here it is: 14 miles from Burnham to Bradwell, all but a couple of them along the wall that prevents the North Sea reclaiming large parts of the Dengie Hundred. When the older wall gave way before the great tide of 1953, a watcher at the northern end said it sounded 'like a clap of thunder'.

The marshland fields behind the modern sea defences are still heavily veined by drainage ditches, leading through a series of outfalls, each named after its respective farm. In the days when winkles were a more widely appreciated delicacy, little 'winkle brigs' from West Mersea would lie in the outfalls while their crews searched the Dengie flats for

The high street in Burnham.

the shellfish. At the right times of year great flocks of migrating birds drift along this shore, but if you want to study them go there on a rising tide that will drive the waders up over the saltings.

Marked on my Ordnance Survey map is a 'decoy pond' attached to Marsh House farm, relic of a type of wildfowling that has been illegal since 1954, but was once widespread and profitable. At its peak there were about a hundred decoy ponds along the East Coast, providing an estimated half million ducks a year – widgeon, mallard, teal, pintail and so on – for Leadenhall and the other markets.

From above, a decoy pond looked a bit like an octopus: a stretch of water with a number of winding, tapered arms leading off it, each covered at the end by a tunnel of hooped netting. A path ran alongside each arm, partially screened from birds sitting on the water. Living on the pond were a group of well-fed tame ducks, who would respond to the decoyman's whistle and whose role it was to tempt their wild companions down one of the deadly blind alleys. As his tame ducks gradually led their brethren into the trap, the decoyman's well trained, sandy coloured dog would show itself running between the screens like a fox, prompting the wild ducks to lunge forward in a mobbing impulse to drive it away. Finally the man himself would jump out behind the wild birds, at which they would take off in alarm and fly quite literally into a dead end.

If a pond was well sited and skilfully run, a marshland farmer could reckon to recover the cost of digging it and rigging the nets in its first season. Back in 1714, one of the ponds on the Dengie, at Steeple, caught 6,296 widgeon in that single year. But there are no longer any commercial decoy ponds, any more than there are professional wildfowlers. In Essex, I understand, this curious form of mass slaughter ceased in the 1940s.

When I came to live in this part of the world I was told a story about the Dengie: how in the old days farmers down there would get through several young wives in a lifetime because their brides, bred on the 'uplands' of Maldon or Danbury, rapidly succumbed to malarial marsh fever, the ague, and had to be replaced. I always assumed the story had been passed on from Victorian times by word of mouth, but on checking a reference in Daniel Defoe's *A Tour Through the Whole Island of Great*

Britain, published in 1724, I found it there. Even then Defoe was not writing from direct observation, but merely quoting some old boy he had evidently met in a local alehouse – as professional hacks have done through the centuries. As one would expect from the author of *Robinson Crusoe* and *Moll Flanders* his version of the tale is much more richly embellished than the one I heard, so let me quote him:

'I have one remark more, before I leave this damp part of the world, and which I cannot omit on the women's account; namely, that I took notice of a strange decay of the sex here; insomuch, that all along this county it was very frequent to meet with men that had had from five or six, to fourteen or fifteen wives; nay, and some more; and I was inform'd that in the marshes on the other side of the river over against Candy Island, there was a farmer, who was then living with the five-and-twentieth wife, and that his son, who was but about 35 years old, had already had about fourteen; indeed this part of the story I only had by report, tho' by good hands too; but the other is well known, and easie to be inquired in to about Fobbing, Curringham, Thundersley, Benfleet, Prittlewell, Wakering, Great Stambridge, Cricksea, Burnham, Dengy, and other towns of the like situation.

'The reason, as a merry fellow told me, who said he had had about a dozen and a half of wives (tho' I found afterwards he fibb'd a little) was this: that they being bred in the marshes themselves, and seson'd to the place, did pretty well with it; but that they always went up into the hilly country, or to speak their own language, into the uplands for a wife: that when they took the young lasses out of the wholesome and fresh air, they were healthy, fresh and clean, and well; but when they came out of their native air into the marshes among the fogs and damps, there they presently chang'd their complexion, got an ague or two, and seldom held it above half a year, or a year at the most; and then, said he, we go to the uplands again, and fetch another; so that marrying of wives was reckon'd a kind of good farm to them.

'It is true, the fellow told this in a kind of drollery, and mirth; but the fact, for all that, is certainly true; and that they have abundance of wives by that very means.'

Life on the Dengie is no longer that exciting. It's still a strange place, however, naturally isolated by its geography just as Foulness Island, on the other side of the Crouch, is artificially cut off by the military checkpoints. The mixture of dogged independence and introverted loyalty one finds in these Essex communities is symbolised by a little slate-roofed chapel at Tillingham, right in the heart of the Dengie. It was the last chapel dedicated to the Peculiar People, an austere local sect whose name comes from the biblical usage – as in Paul's epistle to Titus, where he refers to Christ's intention to 'purify unto himself a peculiar people, zealous

The Peculiar People's chapel at Tillingham.

of good works'. All the other remaining congregations of the Peculiar People changed their name to the 'Union of Evangelical Churches', thinking it would sound more attractive to the youngsters they hoped to recruit. Tillingham stuck out against this concession to public relations.

Sadly, at the time of writing the chapel is up for sale. Years ago, when talking to the elderly man who looked after it, he made some remark about the end of the world not being far off. For a moment I thought he might be warning of a disastrous accident at the nearby Bradwell nuclear power station. But it turned out to be another biblical reference – something about the barns being full after a good harvest.

Bradwell nuclear power station.

THE BLACKWATER

BRADWELL – STONE – OSEA ISLAND – MALDON – HEYBRIDGE – GOLDHANGER

THE BLACKWATER IS the largest estuary between the Thames and the Wash, and from a sailing point of view perhaps the finest. The entrance off Bradwell is more than a mile wide, though there is an invisible navigational bottleneck further offshore. Inland it stretches broad and deep for about five miles, and for another five miles past the islands of Osea and Northey to the ancient port of Maldon at the head of the tidal river.

The Blackwater has never been an empty estuary, left alone with its seabirds. From Roman times at least, mankind has been busy along its shores. But fortunately for those of us who live there now it has not been overwhelmed by any one form of maritime activity. Commercial shipping, fishing, oyster farming, yachting and wildfowling have all contributed to its character.

Two buildings within sight of one another on the Bradwell shore, both in their time useful navigational landmarks, symbolise its breadth of history. The plain stone chapel of St Peter's-on-the-Wall, on the seaward extremity of Sales Point, stands on the foundations of the Roman fort of Othona. Just along the sea wall is Bradwell's decommissioned nuclear power station, two great blocks of concrete, steel and glass which each housed a uranium-fuelled reactor, heating steam to generate electricity.

St Peter's has looked out over these marshes since AD 654. It was built by St Cedd, who sailed south from Lindisfarne as a missionary to the East Saxons at the invitation of King Sigbert. Evidently a practical man, Cedd erected his chapel on the solid foundations provided by the main western gate of the ruined Othona fort. So that straight road you take to reach the chapel from the eastern outskirts of Bradwell village has been trodden by many Roman soldiers as well as Christian pilgrims – the latter still visiting in large numbers. Othona was one of a chain of defensive estuarial forts commanded by Carausius, 'the Count of the Saxon Shore', which included Walton-next-Felixstowe (submerged off Harwich), Burgh Castle (behind Yarmouth), Brancaster (on the north Norfolk coast) and possibly Dunwich (also submerged).

As you can see from the flat red Roman bricks marking the shape of former arches, Cedd's builders also found plenty of material among the ruins. His church originally had a curved apse, whose shape can be traced in the grass on the seaward side, separated from the nave by three narrow arches with a small room on either side. At the other end of the nave there was a small tower, which must have made it a more prominent navigation mark for ships entering the estuary.

But just as the abandoned imperial fortress became the raw material of Cedd's missionary zeal, so his church was in time overtaken by domestic economy. The medieval village of Bradwell grew further inland, where a new parish church was built in the 14th century. Cedd's physical work became redundant, staring out over the marshes much as it does today, though the long straight sea wall that stretches away south to such dramatic effect would not have been there then. By the 17th century St Peter's had become a barn – you can see where the nave wall was demolished to make way for the farm carts – and it stayed like that until 1920 when it was given back to the diocese.

Meanwhile somebody else had found a practical use for a corner of the old fort. The tiny black weatherboarded cottage facing the east wind from behind the modern sea wall, otherwise sheltered only by a cluster of neglected fruit trees, was the home of Walter Linnett, last of the professional wildfowlers. For some years after the Second World War he was still earning a living punt-gunning and eel-spearing. I never met him myself, but by one of the happier chances of a Dutch cruise I once made, the yacht that whisked mine to safety from beneath the descending span of a vast motorway bridge came from West Mersea. And chatting later over a thank-you drink, someone must have mentioned wildfowling because the owner remembered Walter Linnett coming 'on his holidays' to the White Hart, and regaling the Mersea youngsters with tall tales of the ducks he shot over the marshes and the eels he caught in his thigh boots while wading to retrieve them.

The Bradwell cottage is said to be haunted by the figure of an old seaman. Perhaps it is Walter Linnett's father or grandfather, who both lived there. If so, one wonders what he makes of the Essex Birdwatching Society's members who now use the cottage as an observatory, wielding telescopes rather than shotguns. The arc of sand beyond the saltings opposite is known as the Bradwell Cockle Spit reserve and visitors are asked not to disturb it.

As an alternative to the Romans' road back to Bradwell, one can take the two mile walk round the sea wall past the old military airfield and the abandoned nuclear power station. In terms of the nuclear power industry's brief history, the Bradwell station is already something of a monument. Commissioned in 1962, it was one of the first pair of full-scale gas-cooled Magnox stations to be built in this country, now gradually being dismantled as the radiation fades. Unless it is eventually replaced by an equally prominent, brightly lit structure, it will be missed by sailors who use it to find their way into an otherwise thinly marked estuary. The steel structure in the river immediately opposite the station, where yachts and fishing boats often lie at anchor, was the cooling water intake.

Past the power station, the sea wall turns in along Bradwell Creek and brings you back to the road opposite the Green Man pub on

Bradwell waterside. (If you take a drink at the pub, try deciphering the cryptic sign above the old fireplace.) The creek now has a marina, but small craft still launch off the shingle hard at the bottom of the road past the Bradwell Quay Yacht Club. A few of the twisted posts that made it a primitive sort of quay, 'the old men of Bradwell', can still be seen. This was the home port of the smartly turned out Parker fleet of sailing barges which included the racer *Veronica*, some say the fastest barge ever built.

Three miles upriver is a steep shingle bank known simply as 'the Stone'. Stone Sailing Club's racing dinghies share this convenient launching beach with water skiers and large powerboats. The waterside pub is also a good vantage point from which to watch the start of the annual races for sailing barges and 'old gaffers', the older fashioned gaff-rigged yachts and fishing smacks.

A mile or so further and the river narrows between Stansgate Point, family home of the politician Tony Benn, and Osea Island. Here the ebb tide fairly sluices past. Osea can be reached at low tide along a causeway on the northwestern side (postal collections used to be 'according to tide'). But the island is privately owned farmland, so strangers are not welcome except on the foreshore. The steepest beach is on the southern side just below the little derelict pier and this is a favourite yacht anchorage, especially for boats that have come down from Maldon just for one tide.

A few elderly yachtsmen recall the 'Barnacle', a massive post set into Osea beach by the Heybridge ironfounder Edward Bentall to lean his revolutionary 110-foot yawl *Jullanar* against for scrubbing. Bentall was an agricultural engineer who had developed a new sort of plough and was also interested in experimental yachts. With the Wivenhoe designer John Harvey, he produced in 1875 what was arguably this country's first modern sailing yacht. Her hull had a boldly cutaway forefoot and smoothly tucked canoe stern, quite different from the long-keeled straight-stemmers then fashionable. *Jullanar* was known somewhat derisively as 'Bentall's plough' but she turned out to be a successful racer.

Her owner had meanwhile taken his ideas a stage further with a smaller design called *Evolution,* which had a short, deep, bulb keel – unfortunately combined with a thoroughly contemporary plank-on-edge hull rather than the beamy shape that would support such a keel today. As a result she was a failure, but much of the thinking that went into her was scientifically sound (a hundred years ahead of its time) as the shapes of today's racing yachts demonstrate. You will find the full story in John Leather's book about this estuary, *The Salty Shore.*

Sail past Osea pier with a local yachtsman and he will be sure to tell you the story of the fine house that stands behind it. Pier and house were built by Fred Charrington of the London brewing family as part of a scheme to turn Osea into the Edwardian equivalent of a health farm, a place where alcoholics could dry out. It seems Charrington conceived the idea after watching a woman outside an East End pub pleading with her husband to come home, only to get a thump across the head for her trouble. As the drunkard retreated to the bar again, the brewer looked up and saw his own name on the sign.

Maldon, at any rate, was appreciative of Charrington's guilty conscience. Cook's boatyard helped build the pier and fitted out a little steamboat called the *Annie* to run trips from the town. Local fishermen were meanwhile sabotaging the good work by running cargoes of illicit booze ashore on the island in the best East Coast smuggling tradition, or so the story goes. The house by the pier, incidentally, was known locally as 'the Doctor's house', which explains why the little green starboard-hand buoy which marks the shoal off that corner of Osea is still called The Doctor.

There used to be a large heronry at the western end of the island until it became a casualty of Dutch elm disease. Watching those lanky birds clinging on among the skeletal branches of dying elms, one could trace the progress over several seasons of a pest that largely destroyed one of the glories of the Essex skyline.

During the First World War Osea established one of the Blackwater's few links with the Royal Navy. The island became the base for a remarkable breed of Thorneycroft motor torpedo boats and minelayers, long slender craft with rolled decks reputedly capable of more than 50 knots. They were hauled out across that same beach just downstream of the pier, where you can see the remains of their slipways.

During the Second World War the former Cardnell's yard at the head of Lawling Creek opposite built motor launches and torpedo boats. But these were tame creatures compared with the grey shapes that would swoop out from under the Osea shore in 1918, to embark on daring raids across the North Sea – the sort of thing Erskine Childers would have loved.

Northey, the last island dividing the river before it reaches Maldon, is connected with a much earlier war, between marauding bands of mainly Danish Vikings and the Saxons – in this case the East Saxons we remember in the name Essex. In 991 the island was the setting for the Battle of Maldon, which we know about from a heroic Old English poem containing so much vivid detail that the author must either have been there or heard accounts from some who were.

The battle was fought at a time when the Danes were ranging up and down the East Coast in their longships, threatening to ravage one coastal community after another unless they were paid off in Danegeld. The fleet which sailed up the Blackwater, or the Pant as it was called in those days, had just come from sorting out Ipswich, according to the Anglo-Saxon Chronicle. And it may have been led by one of the great Viking warriors, Olaf Tryggvason, who later became King of Norway. The Saxons, at any rate, were prepared to fight rather than pay protection money and called on their own champion, Bryhtnoth, Earldorman of Essex, to challenge the invaders.

Bryhtnoth was renowned as a fighting man, partly no doubt because he was nearly seven feet tall, and politically he was one of the most important men in England. But by that time he was old, and not as quick as he would have liked with the heavy sword seen on his statue outside All Saints Church in Maldon (another, more modern statue stands at the end of the promenade); and he possessed a fatal sense of military honour. It was this last trait that let him and the Saxons down, because they were up against professional pirates. Yet at the same time it was the honourable way in which Bryhtnoth conducted the losing battle, fighting to the death with his faithful retainers in accordance with the Germanic military code (though others did run away when they saw him cut down), that inspired perhaps the finest Old English poem to survive.

Bryhtnoth's tactical error was to let the Viking 'war wolves' cross the tidal causeway from Northey to the mainland and form up, before joining battle with them. When the invaders first called across demanding tribute, the Saxon champion sarcastically suggested that it would be a shame for them to have come so far in search of English silver and gold without being offered a fight. One of the East Saxon warriors then struck down the first Viking to venture across the causeway as the tide went down. But at that crucial point, 'overswayed by his heart's arrogance' as the poet puts it, Bryhtnoth yielded to the Vikings' crafty appeals for a fair fight on dry land: 'The war wolves waded across, mourned not for the water'. Early in the battle the Essex champion was wounded by a spear, which one of his men promptly hurled back to kill its owner. Then another blow almost severed Bryhtnoth's sword arm and the battle of Maldon was as good as lost. (When his long skeleton was disinterred from the wall of Ely Cathedral in the 18th century the collar bone had indeed been almost cut through – and they never found his head!)

Similar contests between gentlemen and players, amateurs and professionals, have been fought out on many occasions since, usually with similar results. From this safe distance in time, the nice thing about the Battle of Maldon is that the topography, which was also so important

All that remains of the sailing barge Gipping at Northey.

to the outcome, has scarcely changed in a thousand years. It has admittedly been suggested that the battle was fought across Heybridge Creek, along what is still known as 'The Causeway' from Maldon, but what I have seen of the evidence points much more strongly to Northey. There has been a half-tide causeway on the western side since Roman times, as indicated in the poem; it is the obvious place for the Vikings to have run their boats ashore as they came in sight of the Saxon fortress on Maldon hill. They would have made camp on the island's only high ground, overlooking the end of the causeway.

If you want to work it out for yourself, either park a car by the terraced cottages on the Mundon road and take the footpath down past South House Farm, or follow the sea wall round from the end of Maldon promenade. Northey Island, or what is left of it after the sea wall collapsed, is now managed as a nature reserve by the National Trust. Occasionally there is an open day, when hundreds of visitors put on their wellies and trudge across the shingle causeway. For the rest of the year it is left to the gulls, the waders and the short-eared owls.

From Northey, the river winds through a series of right-angled bends to Maldon's Hythe Quay, often referred to simply as 'the Hythe'. This is the place to take a close look at some of the remaining Thames sailing barges that once linked ports, creeks and harbours all along the East Coast. You will probably find half a dozen of them rafted neatly alongside, brown spritsails furled high above their decks, the 'bobs' on their still loftier topmasts fluttering in the breeze coming over the hill.

The Northey causeway.

A lovely old town, Maldon. Rambling and dishevelled in the Essex way, it combines many of the ingredients that make a community worthwhile: to earn its living, a mixture of industry, farming, shopkeeping and recreational boating, plus a bit of fishing; a sense of history but nothing obsessive; in general a tolerant blend of people, activities, pubs and churches; a non-conformist kind of place that is big enough, in every sense, to accept a few peculiar people without fuss.

Maldon's name means 'the hill marked by a cross'. The town grew up round the site of a hilltop fortress overlooking the first place at which the estuary could easily be forded or bridged. This was at the confluence of two small rivers, the Chelmer and the Blackwater (known to the Saxons as the Pant, a fact I discovered not by reading Old English but because

The Promenade at Maldon.

my first cruising yacht was a little Blackwater Sloop built at Maldon by Dan Webb & Feesey and called *Panta*).

Approaching by road off the A12 Chelmsford bypass, you enter the town at the top of the High Street, the site of the original Saxon 'burgh'. To the left, at the bottom of one of the steepest hills in Essex, is the Fullbridge river crossing. To the right the High Street slopes more gently towards the quayside. This top end of the town contains many of the important old buildings, including All Saints Church with its unique triangular 13th century tower and, by the porch, a statue of local hero Bryhtnoth (the Saxons would have spelt it 'Byrhtnoth', by the way). Opposite is the Blue Boar, which has been an inn since 1573, and just beyond, the Moot Hall with its town clock and five chiming bells on the roof. The projecting wooden porch from 1830 disguises a 15th century brick building known then as D'Arcy's Tower – worth looking round if you can, for its Plantagenet spiral brick staircase and the miniature courtroom on the first floor that used to feed a dungeon in the basement.

Further down the High Street on the left, the former church of St Peter's houses the 18th century Plume Library, including first editions of Milton's *Paradise Lost* and Spenser's *Faerie Queene*. The imposing house immediately beyond it was once the home of Edward Bright, 'the largest man who ever lived on this island', who had an 83-inch waist and weighed 42 stones before he died at the age of 29. From there the shops curve round towards the waterside church of St Mary's, whose little wooden steeple is the shape that first catches the eye if you are sailing up the river.

The first substantial building on the quayside is the black shed of the old Cook's boatyard, usually with two or three sailing barges alongside for repairs. The special skills of shaping and fastening the great baulks of timber that go into a sailing barge have been practised here at least since 1895, when Walter Cook started work on the *Dawn*, the firm's first order.

It's often said of aircraft designs that if they look right, they fly right. The Thames barge is a superb demonstration of almost the opposite principle – that a vessel designed perfectly to fulfil its working function will also be aesthetically satisfying. There can be no doubt about the beauty of a sailing barge, whether at close quarters alongside the quay or merely glimpsed as an inverted wedge of dark sail against the estuary skyline, but it evolved from the humble Thames lighter simply to do a job of work. The broad, shallow, flat-bottomed hull meant cheaper construction, easy loading and the ability to sail empty without ballast. A vessel like this was equally at home working the London docks, punching her way down the coast or wriggling into some marshland creek. At low tide she could sit safely on sand or mud. A pair of Dutch-style leeboards bolted to her sides acted as lifting keels. The permanently rigged sprit enabled a heavy tanned mainsail to be left permanently aloft, if necessary brailed up with the topsail still set above it to catch the breeze above tall wharves or trees. Yet the whole rig could be lowered to shoot a bridge, and above all, a 150 ton, 80 foot seagoing vessel could be handled by two men.

No wonder the East Coast barge fleet was once counted in thousands, a few of which were still trading years after the Second World War when steam and diesel power had long since killed off less efficient forms of commercial sail. It is because of that efficiency that some are still around as yachts and charter craft, sailed and lived in, not dead specimens in a maritime museum.

Maldon's barging speciality were the 'stackies', perhaps the most remarkable adaptation of all and an obvious justification for that link between plough and sail celebrated on several East Coast pub signs. They were made especially flat and broad to take a complete haystack built halfway up the mainmast. Encumbered like that, they would sail right up the London River, often above the bridges, where they would offload the hay as feed for the city horses and then complete the ecological cycle by returning to the farm quay with a cargo of straw and dung.

Walking northwards along the Hythe, past the clubhouse of the Maldon Little Ship Club, the next building on the waterside is a beacon for which many local sailors steer, the Queen's Head. Beyond that is a former sailmaking loft, and finally the boatyard at the bottom of North

Street, whose ship and boat building tradition probably goes back at least to the 17th century. Maldon was a major port providing warships for the Navy, and this is considered the most likely site from which the 50-gun frigate *Jersey* was launched in 1654. She fought the Dutch at the Battle of Sole Bay, and is also notable as having been commanded – on paper, though never in reality – by the diarist Samuel Pepys. He was appointed as a formality so that he qualified to attend a court martial.

By the late 19th century John Howard had taken the yard (his small square house still stands beside it), applying his artistry to barges like the *Ethel Maud* and the *Mirosa*. Then between the wars it was yachts, particularly the little 18 foot Blackwater Sloops, an East Coast equivalent of the South Coast's Hillyard 2½-tonners.

In the 19th century the port of Maldon developed further upstream, just below the Fullbridge at the end of a charming Thomas-the-Tank-Engine kind of railway line from Witham. That connection fell foul of Beeching. The seagoing coasters that eased their way through the crowded moorings to bring grain or animal feed to the mills on the north bank – reducing the yachts to the scale of toys – have also gone. The former timber wharf is derelict. As I write, residential 'development' is imminent. But there is still plenty of activity at this end of the harbour, where a rich assortment of vessels awaits refit, repair, conversion, or a turn in the dry dock.

On the south bank is the Maldon crystal salt works, one of the few things, along with the Viking battle, for which the town is widely known in other parts of the country. Of the three sea salt manufacturers in the UK this is the oldest, a family concern established in 1882 and now run by the fourth generation of Osbornes. The simple, black, weatherboarded factory is built on the site of a 12th century salt pan, then one of hundreds along the Essex rivers, when salt was one of the few ways of preserving food. One explanation for the mysterious 'red hills' of Essex is that they are the remains of burnt earthenware pots in which brine was evaporated to make salt. A familiar inn sign in this part of the world is the Three Cups, representing the armorial bearings of the ancient Salter's Company.

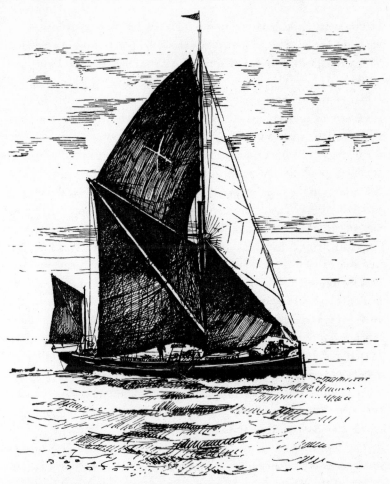

Once there were thousands ... the sailing barge Marjorie.

The Blackwater is one of the saltiest estuaries in Britain because there are wide mudflats and saltings on which the sea water can evaporate, drying easterly winds, and relatively little fresh water rainfall to dilute the accumulating salt. To make Maldon salt today, water is pumped from the river, filtered and boiled in 10-foot square stainless steel vats. The liquor is then left to simmer until crystals claimed to be unique to this process begin to form on the surface. Each crystal, of whatever size, appears quite suddenly in the shape of an inverted pyramid, fills and sinks. After 15 or 16 hours the vat is full of crystalline salt which is delicately 'drawn' with wooden rakes and shovelled out for drying and packing.

Above the Fullbridge there are footpaths on both sides of the river. The easy one to find starts from behind the riverside pub and follows the top of the sea wall to Beeleigh Falls, the weirs at the confluence of the rivers Chelmer and Blackwater, above which the Chelmer is canalised as far as Chelmsford. From the falls you can either return to Maldon on the other bank, past what remains of the 12th century Beeleigh Abbey (now a beautifully secluded private house), or turn back towards Heybridge along the Chelmer & Blackwater Navigation. The canal winds through the village to emerge under Wave Bridge, carrying the B1022 road alongside the handsome great warehouse built by Bentall in 1863, and then runs for a straight mile across the fields to Heybridge Basin.

This long detour round Maldon to a sea lock halfway down Colliers Reach was quite deliberate. The merchants who built the canal in 1798 wanted to break Maldon's monopoly and avoid its tolls. From then on colliers and timber ships could unload into lighters for shipment inland as far as the county town of Chelmsford. Some Heybridge funerals were also waterborne to the canalside cemetery, a stately horse-drawn lighter serving for hearse and carriages.

The fact that the canal and its lock basin were conceived to do Maldon down bred an enmity between the neighbouring ports as keen as any on the East Coast. Although the ancient village of Heybridge is Maldon's twin at the other end of the Causeway, the 'basiners' are another matter. 'Heybridge cannibals' the Maldon men used to call them, a bitter reference to the fact that some of the older Basin families are apparently descended from the 'navigators' who built the usurping canal and then settled alongside it.

Heybridge is no longer a commercial harbour, though a few fishing boats make their home there. Timber lightering did revive after the Second World War, but the laborious transhipment from ships lying downriver became uneconomic. Even the Dutch eel storage barges have gone, though until recently at least there seemed to be plenty of eels in the canal; you could see the elvers struggling to surmount Beeleigh weirs. What remains is a recreational waterway whose basin is always filled with a marvellous variety of yachts, barges and smacks, usually including a few elegant, deep-draft old-timers who would not otherwise be able to berth this far up the estuary. So it's well worth turning off the B1026 (the lower Maldon–Colchester road) to browse along the canal or test the beer at one of the two pubs, especially if it's high tide and boats are on the move locking in and out.

Heybridge has sensibly provided visitors with a car park giving direct access to the canalside and this is as good a place as any to begin one of the many sea wall walks the Blackwater offers. Turn north at the lock and the wall takes you past the Blackwater Sailing Club (one of its founders was the owner of *Jullanar*, Edward Bentall) whose green flashing clubhouse light helps lead boats up the river from Osea on a dark night.

Beyond the clubhouse you skirt a small creek that once served the Saltcote maltings, for which the sailing barge *Saltcote Belle* was built at

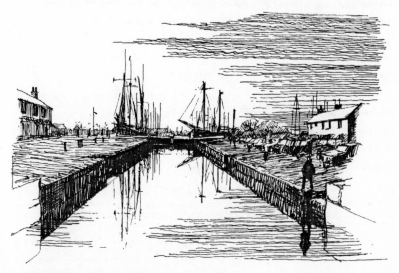

Heybridge Basin, built to rival Maldon.

Howard's Maldon yard. From there the wall follows Mill Beach, where the long established caravan plots are tended as carefully as any cottage garden, to Decoy Point and the landward end of the causeway laid down by the Romans to reach Osea Island.

The broad flats behind the island are known as The Stumble. It's a popular two mile walk round to Goldhanger, usually enlivened in winter by flocks of geese though in nothing like the numbers that must have been present at the turn of the century, when they were said to darken the sky for half a mile, sounding like 'fifty packs of hounds in full cry'. Nowadays they are mostly black brents, and with the estuary stripped of eelgrass local farmers are glumly aware that a drifting flock is as likely to settle on the landward side of the wall as it is on the mud to seaward.

At Goldhanger ('grassland where the corn marigold grows') the head of the creek has been reclaimed to form a small recreation ground, from the far end of which Fish Street leads to the warmth of the Chequers, next to St Peter's Church. This north shore of the estuary is indented with little gutways that serve little purpose now but to force yet another detour in the meandering sea wall, but once provided farm landings for the barges and, in the early 19th century particularly, quiet corners from which smuggled cargoes of Dutch gin or French brandy could be worked up through the lanes to Tiptree Heath and beyond.

A gun punt.

MERSEA ISLAND

TOLLESBURY – SALCOTT – THE STROOD – WEST MERSEA – EAST MERSEA

'BETWEEN THE MOUTHS of the Blackwater and the Colne, on the east coast of Essex, lies an extensively marshy tract veined and freckled in every part with water. It is a wide waste of debatable ground contested by sea and land, subject to incessant incursions from the former, but stubbornly maintained by the latter.' With this description the Reverend Sabine Baring-Gould began his melodramatic novel of the Essex marshes, *Mehalah.* He could hardly have done otherwise, because without some understanding of the desolate world of creeks, mud, fleets and saltings through which his characters moved, readers would not have been able to follow the narrative.

Baring-Gould himself was a relative stranger to this area, a West Countryman best known through his hymn 'Onward Christian Soldiers'. He spent only ten years in the draughty vicarage at East Mersea, from 1871. But his journals show what an impact they made on him: the incessant wind, the stench of rotting sprats used to manure the fields, the mosquitoes, the curious dialect, the poverty, the tension between the static farming communities and the more outward looking waterside villages like West Mersea, where the blue guernsey and red fisherman's cap of his wild half-gypsy heroine Mehalah would not look out of place. Yet he conceded that the marshes were 'not without beauty' and took some pains to observe and record it:

'In summer, the thrift mantles the marshes with shot satin, passing through all gradations of tint from maiden's blush to lily white. Thereafter a purple glow steals over the waste, as the sea lavender bursts into flower, and simultaneously every creek and pool is royally fringed with sea aster. A little later the glass-wort, that shot up green and transparent as emerald glass in the early spring, turns to every tinge of carmine.'

Mehalah has often been compared to *Wuthering Heights*. But perhaps the closer parallel is with the Reverend Cobbold's *History of Margaret Catchpole,* about an equally strong-willed woman, 'as fearless as a Newmarket jockey', who rode through the Suffolk heathland in the same romantic style that Baring-Gould's heroine drove her boat across the Essex skyline. Strong Victorian meat, but still appreciated round here.

My own favourite story of Mehalah's creator, an immensely energetic man who had fifteen children and wrote 159 books, pictures him standing at his church door after the service, as vicars do, exchanging a brief word or two with each member of the congregation as they file out:

'And who's little girl are you?' he asks, bending down to pat the small creature pulling at his surplice. 'Yours, Daddy,' she replies.

Approaching Mehalah's marshland along the north shore of the Blackwater, you come first to Tollesbury, at the head of a creek running off Mersea Quarters behind the Nass sand. Old Hall marshes lie to the north of the twin channels, with Tollesbury Wick to the south. Boats reach Tollesbury's tidal marina along a narrow gutway – which

Boat stores at Tollesbury.

has nevertheless floated some really big yachts in its time – known as Woodrolfe Creek.

By road the approach is along the B1023 from Tolleshunt D'Arcy, which leads into the small village square. Visitors interested in Tollesbury's maritime heritage can conveniently park here and step inside the medieval parish church to view the unique Seafarers' Window. The lurid colours may not be to everyone's taste, but the window is a remarkable record of the fact that for several decades this tiny marshland village was at the forefront of the international yachting scene.

Tollesbury came to yachting later than Brightlingsea or Wivenhoe on the River Colne. But by the turn of the century many of the Blackwater men had adopted a similar working pattern: fishing through the winter, then taking a berth as a professional yacht hand for the summer. As Tollesbury crew members progressed to become skippers, they would bring the yachts they sailed home for the winter, to be laid up and refitted. So the local boatyard also prospered.

All this activity reached its peak just before the First World War, which is when the fine row of wooden boat stores was built down by the waterside. One of the largest vessels ever to wriggle her way up Woodrolfe Creek was the 224 ton schooner *Heartsease,* floated into a mud berth at Tollesbury in 1951, but minus her lead keel – which substantially reduced her original 13½ foot draft. This faded but still opulent Edwardian beauty was dug out again by enthusiasts from the Royal Norfolk and Suffolk Yacht Club in 1968 and towed to Lowestoft for restoration.

At about the time *Heartsease* first took to the water, work began on the Kelvedon & Tollesbury Light Railway, the 'Crab and Winkle'. The first train ran down the line through Tiptree and Tolleshunt D'Arcy in 1904. For Tollesbury it meant that fish could be sent straight up to Billingsgate, and London yachtsmen would be encouraged to keep their boats in the creek. The next stage, completed in 1907, was an extension of the railway round the back of the village, where its remains can still be identified, to end at a wooden pier on the main estuary of the Blackwater. The village began to imagine itself not only as a fashionable yachting centre, to rival Brightlingsea on the Colne, but perhaps even as a Continental packet station.

The First World War put an end to such dreams. The pier extension was closed in 1921 and the whole of the railway in 1951. But the involvement of Tollesbury men in yacht racing on a grand scale, and particularly in repeated efforts to win back the America's Cup, continued through the inter-war years.

That story is recorded in the stained glass of the Seafarers' Window, donated by a local man, Frederick Hasler, who had emigrated to the United States and become a successful banker. The left hand panel, from the top, shows: the schooner *America,* which started all the trouble in 1851 by winning the Cup in a £100 challenge race round the Isle of Wight; the schooner *Cambria,* which tried to win it back in 1870; *Shamrock,* first of the five challengers built by Sir Thomas Lipton; and *Endeavour,* which mounted the 1934 challenge for T.O.M. Sopwith.

Endeavour was one of the J Class boats, the ultimate development of specialised racing yachts. She was 130 feet long, drew 15 feet with 80 tons of lead on her keel, and set 7,500 square feet of sail on a 170-foot mast. Her spinnaker measured half an acre.

The Js were built like giants' toy yachts, simple things carried to extremes. Those who saw them racing off Harwich and Cowes recall 'a sound like cannon fire' when they luffed into the wind and a ton of cotton mainsail began to shake. *Endeavour* was reckoned the most beautiful of them all, with a powerful sheer and enormous overhangs, her hull painted dark *'Endeavour* blue'. She also came closer than any British challenger to recovering the America's Cup; even the defenders acknowledged that she was faster than the American *Rainbow.* She won the first two races of their series in 1934 and but for a controversial near-collision (after which she was ruled to have hoisted her protest flag 'too slowly') she might well have carried off the trophy instead of leaving it to the Australians half a century later.

Although the yachting world into which the Js were launched came to an end with the outbreak of the Second World War, there is no need to write of them entirely in the past tense. Half a century later I was able to join a completely restored *Velsheda* on Southampton Water, leaving a startled motor coaster in her wake as she surged past at 15 knots. In 1979 *Endeavour's* rusting hull was dug out of a mud berth to be rebuilt on Calshot Spit. Several other Js restored to working order found berths in Italy and the United States, and they periodically meet to race.

The immediate relevance of *Endeavour* in Tollesbury's church window is that she was skippered for a while by a local man, Captain Edward Heard. He took her to the US in 1937 as a trials boat for Sopwith's *Endeavour II,* and beat both *Rainbow* and the new American defender *Ranger* in the preliminary races. On the way home *Endeavour* broke loose from the motor yacht that was towing her through hurricane force winds, and having lost radio contact was presumed sunk. Two and a half weeks later she came storming up the Channel under her cut-down yawl rig and was given a triumphal reception in Portsmouth.

There was also a good deal of celebrating that night in the Kings Head at Tollesbury.

The right hand panel of the Seafarers' Window shows, again from the top: a 'billy-boy', that is a primitive type of clinker-built coaster that disappeared in the early years of the century; a ketch-rigged barge; a 'stackie', which was a spritsail barge adapted to carry stacks of straw and hay to London from the Essex farms; and a Colchester registered oyster smack of the kind that worked out of the nearby creeks between the wars.

Before you leave the church take a look at the font, bought in 1718 with a five pound fine (a vast sum at the time) imposed on a parishioner who turned up to the service drunk and disorderly. It bears the explanatory inscription, rather carelessly carved, on the churchwarden's orders: 'Good people all I pray take Care That in ye Church you doe not Sware As this man Did'.

To reach the waterside, drive through the village and fork left down Woodrolfe Road, lined with small brick villas built in Tollesbury's most expansive period. The road ends on a shingle hard with a marina on the right; its water is contained behind a sill at low tide while the creek runs away to the left. Tollesbury's cruising club is also based at the marina and indeed nowadays the waterfront is mainly devoted to the requirements of weekend yachting. But as in other Essex harbours, the uniformity of the modern fibreglass is relieved by a rich variety of traditional wooden craft, obsolete racers, work boats and hulks. In this part of the world they appreciate the older woman. The Blackwater smack *Boadicea,* which spent a hundred years of her long life working out of Woodrolfe Creek, was built at Maldon in 1808 and is still going strong, albeit almost completely rebuilt.

From Tollesbury waterside you may take the sea wall in either direction for longish walks round the neighbouring marshes. To the southeast the wall skirts Tollesbury Wick, another bird reserve, run by the Essex Wildlife Trust, which includes avocets among its attractions. Returning along the estuary shore, you can leave the sea wall at the head of Mill Creek or take the farm road that leads back into the village square past Bohuns Hall. To the northwest, the sea wall winds round numerous watery tentacles reaching inland from Tollesbury Fleet. Beyond that are the extensive Old Hall marshes, bounded on the far side by Salcott Creek. They are managed as a reserve by the Royal Society for the Protection of Birds (whose first autumn report mentioned 4,000 waders, eider duck, bearded tits and a merlin).

I have it on the authority of a Tollesbury friend, Mike Gibson, that these marshes were the setting for an early project by the great 19th century engineer Isambard Kingdom Brunel. Not quite on the scale of the Clifton suspension bridge admittedly, but intriguing none the less. It seems the young Brunel was called down to Tollesbury in about 1830 to build some sort of engine for pumping out the marshes after they had been overwhelmed by a high tide. But being the man he was, he proposed a much simpler solution, a single iron pipe running over the sea wall which, once filled, would continue to siphon the flood water out into Salcott Creek. (There are other accounts of Brunel's visit, but they do not make such a good story.) Ironically, one of the RSPB's first aims on acquiring the marshes was to find some way to raise the water level, for the benefit of the wild fowl.

At the head of the creek lies the tiny village of Salcott-cum-Virley. Salcott just means 'salt cottages' so this was evidently one of the many marshland sites on which medieval salt pans were operated. The water flushing through a network of creeks like this becomes exceptionally saline because salt accumulates through evaporation on the tidal 'saltings' that border the main channels.

Salcott sits on one side of its creek just off the lower road from Maldon to Colchester, the B1026. At one time sailing barges would load hay or deliver coal at the meadow alongside the church, but the head of the creek was dammed off many years ago to prevent flooding. As a boy I used to cycle over to visit a friend there and remember being told that the small window at the back of the cottage, looking down the creek, was once used to signal to smugglers running cargoes across the marsh. I never took the tale seriously, but perhaps I should have done because these remote Essex marshes were popular routes for the secretive style of smuggling that developed in the early 1800s, when the preventive service was making the trade difficult along the more open coasts of Suffolk, Kent and Sussex.

For example Dutch gin might be loaded at Flushing, either into a smack that had sailed across from England or into a fast purpose-built lugger. She would rendezvous among the offshore banks with fishing smacks which could slide unobtrusively into the Mersea channels to dump strings of weighted tubs overboard. Smaller craft ostensibly dredging for oysters could then recover them (unless the Revenue men got there first) and work the cargo inland through villages like Salcott, paying off co-operative farmers and innkeepers on the way.

As you drive into Salcott there is a narrow turning to the left, Mill Lane, which crosses the ditch that used to form the creek and runs alongside it for a couple of hundred yards. At the far end is the old rectory, with the remnants of a second church which once served a separate parish of Virley. It was in Virley church, dilapidated even in those days, that Baring-Gould's Mehalah was married with a heavily symbolic iron ring – promising to obey but not to love or cherish – to the brutal marshland farmer Elijah Rebow. The most colourful character at this grim ceremony was Mrs de Witt, whose fisherman son would have married Mehalah had he not been betrayed by Rebow to the naval press gang. Mrs de Witt was closely modelled on a real person, the ferryman's wife at East Mersea, and Baring-Gould is at his most Dickensian in describing her rumbustious arrival, squeezed into a gown far too small for her and laying about the local yobbos with her umbrella:

'Unable to make the body of the dress meet, she had thrown a smart red coat over it; and having engaged a boy to row her over to Red Hall, sat in the stern, with her skirt pinned over her head, as though the upper part of her person were enveloped in a camera lucida, in which she was viewing in miniature the movements of the outer world . . . Mrs de Witt felt great restraint in the silk gown. Her arms were like wings growing out of her shoulder blades. She was not altogether satisfied that the hooks would hold, and therefore carried to church with her the military coat, over her arm. She wore her hair elaborately frizzled. She had done it with the stove poker, and had worn it for some days in curl papers. Over this was a broad white chip hat, tied under her chin with skyblue ribands, and she had inserted a sprig of forget-me-nots inside the frizzle of hair over her forehead. "Bless my soul," she said to herself, "the boys will go stark staring mad of love at the sight of me. I look like a pretty miss of fifteen – I do, by cock!"'

A mile or two past Salcott, at Great Wigborough, are the headquarters of the Essex Wildlife Trust, and a major nature reserve – where non-members are welcomed – on the northern side of the creek. Here the sea wall has deliberately been breached to create a wetlands habitat and ease the pressure on the area's flood defences – a procedure known as 'managed retreat'. One of the quirkier features of the reserve is a specially protected area for water voles.

The road past Salcott eventually joins the B1025 from Colchester at the Peldon Rose, an exceptionally pretty pub, just before it crosses to Mersea Island. The Roman causeway which carries the road is known as The Strood. At high spring tides it is covered, so Mersea is still a proper island.

To the right of the Strood as you approach the tidal channel, the clump of stunted blackthorn trees that barely break the flat skyline marks Ray Island, where Mehalah is supposed to have lived with her widowed mother. The Ray is owned by the National Trust and managed as a reserve by the Essex Wildlife Trust, reached by a muddy footpath across privately owned saltings.

At the island end of the Strood the road forks left for East Mersea and right for West Mersea, much the larger settlement of the two. The West Mersea church of St Peter and St Paul was built on the site of a Roman villa (you can see some of the flat Roman bricks in the tower) and may well have been another effort by St Cedd, who established the church of St Peter's at Bradwell opposite, also on a Roman site, in 654. The existing tower and its wooden floors date from the 11th century, at about the time Edward the Confessor gave the church to a French abbey in Rouen, in whose ownership it remained until the 15th century. In the 17th century this area was settled by French Huguenots, which is where local names like De Witt, Musset, Rebow and Death come from.

Immediately beyond the church, the main road through the village emerges on the foreshore and follows the creek round to the main hard. The saltings here provide berths for a fine collection of houseboat hulks. Some were magnificent vessels in their day; now they form a decorative line of clipper bows and straight stems, mostly well mantained, each with its own staging and in some cases even a letter box and the equivalent of a garden gate.

Among the most famous – or perhaps one should say notorious – was the concrete schooner *Molliette,* now a wreck marked by a beacon on the Cocum Hills at the edge of the Mersea mudflats. This pioneer of ferro-cement construction made a name for herself early on by knocking a hole in Southend Pier. Between the wars she was run ashore on Mersea beach opposite the Victory pub and used as a club which soon acquired a scandalous reputation. Older residents still recount stories of scantily clad members jumping overboard to avoid a police raid. Finally the Army turned up at the outbreak of the Second World War and had her towed offshore to be scuttled in shallow water as a gunnery target. Somewhere in Mersea is a bungalow named Molliette, built with the proceeds from the thousands of spent shells that were subsequently dredged up round the wreck.

Oyster smacks worked the local grounds under sail until the Second World War.

Anyone who likes boats can spend a pleasant hour or two on West Mersea hard. Mersea was not part of the grand Edwardian yachting scene in the way that Tollesbury was, in part because its sailors were simply too busy dredging for oysters. A fleet of small cutter-rigged oyster smacks worked the local grounds under sail until the Second World War and many of them can still be seen restored as yachts to a condition they hardly knew in their working days, crowding on sail for the annual Old Gaffers race or even doing a bit of trawling. You will see the old oyster pits opposite the Victory, and further along the hard the modern sheds where mature oysters are cleansed and packed. Here too is a famous local institution, the Company Shed – a simple restaurant usually just referred to as 'the Shed' – to which customers bring bread and wine while it provides every kind of seafood. Get there early and beware the scarcity of parking!

West Mersea men also fish offshore (there were 8 registered boats when I last enquired) and nowadays this is by far the busiest yachting centre on the Blackwater. There are two clubs, whose members' interests range all the way from offshore racers to dinghies, and where among the massed fibreglass you may still occasionally come across one of the 14 foot Sprites, her elegant clinker planking showing a family resemblance to the Brightlingsea One-Design and the Walton Jewel, also designed by Robbie Stone.

The former Wyatt's boatyard, now part of Peter Clarke's, began building smacks and turned progressively to yachts. The late William Wyatt – 'Admiral' to the yachting fraternity – was also known for his gun punts, because Mersea was formerly a major centre for wildfowling, both professional and amateur. Indeed the Blackwater has as good a claim as any river on the East Coast to have developed the technique of punt-gunning, more than two hundred years ago, though nowadays only a handful of enthusiasts keep the traditional skills alive.

The earliest punt guns were probably old rampart guns from the Civil War, intended for slaughtering soldiers rather than ducks. Towards the end of the 18th century purpose-built guns were appearing, and by about 1800 they were being mounted on a special type of boat, reputedly introduced by the Buckle family at Maldon. The Essex punt eventually developed as a narrow, flat-bottomed, undecked craft driven by paddles or a sculling oar, and occasionally setting a small spritsail. Under the modern regulations governing wildfowling a motor would not be allowed, but then nobody involved in the sport is likely to want one. They pride themselves on its rigours, compensating for the indiscriminate blunderbuss effect of the great punt gun mounted in the bows by the stealthy patience needed to get within range. Bear in mind that fowling is only allowed along the coast between September and February; the classic setting is a bitter winter's dawn – the colder the better. And since the wildfowl would not normally let a man within gunshot range, the gunner has to lie flat in his punt for long spells, working the tide with oar or paddles but doing his best to look like an innocent, drifting baulk of timber. 'Setting to fowl' they call it. Some birds are now protected: swans,

. . . known as the City since the 19th century.

eider duck, shelduck (which I am told taste awful anyway, even curried) and the black brent, which in Dickens' time was sent up to London by the cartload.

The gun itself is typically about 7 feet long, with perhaps a 1¼ inch bore, firing a 12 ounce charge with a cartridge; though there are still one or two muzzle-loaders around such as the professionals used until the 1950s. Mounted in the bows of the punt, restrained by a short, thick length of rope, the gun leaps upwards and backwards as it fires – the nearest any modern seafarer is likely to come to the sensation of firing an old ship's cannon.

At Mersea, Wyatt built his punts in an old black shed beyond the West Mersea Yacht Club, past Gowen's the sailmakers where the Dabchicks club now stands. I mention this as a way of leading visitors to an exquisitely pretty little group of weatherboarded cottages known as 'Mersea City'; there is even a City Road, with a proper sign. This corner of the island has been known as the City at least since the 19th century. The only place I have come across where the title seemed even

Bawleys at East Mersea.

more unlikely was Longyearbyen, in Spitsbergen, which consists of a few houses perched on stilts at the foot of a glacier.

Fork left instead of right as you leave the Strood and the road leads to East Mersea, an altogether smaller and quieter place. Almost immediately on your left as you climb up from the Strood is Barrow Hill, or Grim's Hoe as it was called in Baring-Gould's time. It's a circular burial mound topped by oak and holly, just behind some railings at the side of the road. The legend is that two Viking brothers, both in love with the same maiden, fought over her until they both died. When the moon was full, it was said, you could hear the clash of swords and the wail of the girl as the warriors renewed their eternal conflict.

The barrow plays an important part in Mehalah's story, because it is while she is there one moonlit night, listening for the sound of the ghostly Vikings, that her house on the Ray is burnt down by her brutal lover Elijah Rebow (whose character was based by Baring-Gould on a Mersea farmer, 'a leading Dissenter', who was believed to have burned down a previous rector's hayricks). Sadly, the legend was not substantiated when the barrow was excavated in 1912. The central burial chamber contained not Viking armour but a glass bowl filled with cremated human bones believed to be of Romano-British origin, dating from the first century AD.

The model for wild Mehalah lived in a cottage at East Mersea and ran off with a soldier from the Colchester garrison. Baring-Gould's rectory was pulled down, apparently made unsafe by the great Essex earthquake of 1884 (in Maldon, a man fell off a ladder) whose epicentre was in the Fingringhoe-Wivenhoe area. His church remains, a simple building with one aisle, entered by a heavily weathered door latched straight into the stone. When I was last there a rather jolly lady, evidently thinking that visitors should be shown the curiosities of the place, pointed out the grave of a fifteen year old girl who had died in 1848, covered with an iron cage to keep bodysnatchers at bay. And I thought of Baring-Gould at work in his study, putting aside next Sunday's sermon and letting his lurid imagination loose on the raw material he found all around him.

Part of the southern shore at the far end of the East Mersea road is managed as a country park. One can leave a car there and walk along the beach, which at high tide provides safe, shingle bathing for young children. At the far end, however, the water swirls deep and fast. This is Mersea Stone and the River Colne; opposite is Brightlingsea Creek. Immediately to your left as you face it, the Pyefleet Channel, famous for its oyster beds, runs back round the island to the Strood. To the northwest, the main channel of the Colne leads to Wivenhoe, Rowhedge and Colchester.

5

THE COLNE

ROWHEDGE – COLCHESTER HYTHE – WIVENHOE – BRIGHTLINGSEA – ST OSYTH

ANY RIVER THAT serves Britain's oldest recorded town is going to have something special about it. At the Bar buoy offshore, ten nautical miles from Colchester, the Colne merges with the Blackwater, but the two adjacent rivers have quite different characters. If I may attempt a dangerous sexual analogy, the broad gentle Blackwater might be described as female, whereas the lean vigorous Colne is quite definitely male. And taking care not to stretch the analogy any further, Colne sailors always seem to have been involved at the forefront of competitive technical development, whether it concerned fishing smacks, grand Edwardian yachts, fast fruit schooners or Olympic catamarans.

It was under Colchester's CK registration that the cutter-rigged Essex smack evolved her final rakish form during the 19th century: straight stem and horizontal bowsprit balanced by a long, low counter stern that was handy for the heavy fishing gear. Maritime historians are agreed that this superlative design owed a lot to cross-fertilisation with the yachts that builders like Sainty and Harvey were producing at Colchester and Wivenhoe.

At Brightlingsea particularly, tucked in just off the estuary, plump little 30-foot smacks that suited the local oyster fishery were also evolved into fast, deep-sea craft of up to twice that size. They ranged far from home, carrying fish for the North Sea herring fleets, dredging scallops on their own account down Channel, fetching lobsters from Norway, stow-boating for winter sprats, or salvaging from clumsier vessels aground on the estuary banks.

It was the Colne men especially who developed the alternating work pattern of winter fishing and summer yachting, later providing many of the professional skippers and crews who challenged for the America's Cup. And their skilled reputation helped generate work for boatyards like Aldous at Brightlingsea. As happened elsewhere, when men came home in the autumn to fit out their smacks for the winter fisheries, some of the big yachts came with them, to be hauled out for refitting or laid up in mud berths along the creek.

The spritsail barges were also a familiar sight in the Colne, though not so many were built there. One extraordinary exception recalled by Hervey Benham in *Down Tops'l* was the lopsided *Exact*, which after being framed up in a field above the Colchester Hythe bridge had one side narrowed by a few inches so that she could 'exactly' squeeze through the bridge piles. Many years later a barge did her best to carry the bridge away altogether when she got stuck under it on a rising tide.

The stretch of river above there was widened in 1867 so that by lowering their mast and sails on deck, seagoing sailing barges could reach East Mills, right in the heart of Colchester. They continued to make this trip until after the Second World War. After poking and pulling their way beneath a second road bridge at the bottom of East Hill, near the

Civil War 'siege house', they would haul the whole rig up again to berth alongside the mills. For a casual observer riding past on a bus, it must have been difficult to work out how on earth these tall vessels got there.

One talks about barges and smacks in the past, but many survive. One of the nice things about the Colne, and still more so the Blackwater, is that so many enthusiasts are prepared to keep these old vessels sailing – and indeed they were working under sail only a generation or two ago. So the clouds of dinghy spinnakers and hard-sheeted overlapping genoas are given perspective by the canted topsails and long, threatening bowsprits of the traditional craft.

Immediately above East Mersea on the west bank of the Colne is the Pyefleet Channel, now a sheltered yacht anchorage but also long associated with the Colchester oyster fishery. The Colchester 'native' is reckoned a queen among oysters. It was highly prized by the Romans, though since then the Essex grounds have often had to be restocked with Portuguese and American varieties. Originally the shellfish were collected haphazardly, wherever they happened to gather on the shingle riverbed. From 1189, when dredging rights were

One in a million young oysters survive to five years.

granted to the burgesses of Colchester, it became a more organised business. By the 19th century many millions of oysters were sold in London through the winter season and the Colne fishery supported a fleet of several hundred smacks. Dredging under sail, though with auxiliary engines, continued until the Second World War. Now only a few powered craft are needed.

The principles of cultivation are unchanged. The oyster bed is cleaned of predators such as starfish and slipper limpets and laid with 'culch', old shells to which the summer's new 'spat' can attach itself. Perhaps one in a million young oysters survive and grow for the minimum five years at which they can be sold, to end their lives sliding down some gourmet's throat. The dredging season runs from September to April, traditionally inaugurated with gin and gingerbread by the Mayor of Colchester.

Above Pyefleet, the shallow Geedon Creek runs in among the Colchester garrison's firing ranges. It is notable only for Rat Island at the entrance, which when the 'bird tides' allow supports the largest nesting colony of black-headed gulls in Essex. Just upstream is the Essex Wildlife Trust's well organised reserve at Fingringhoe Wick (non-members are welcomed, and part of one trail has been adapted for wheelchairs). Road access is from the centre of Fingringhoe village, opposite the church. The reserve was originally created from flooded gravel pits. Nowadays its special attractions include marsh harriers, avocets and up to 40 pairs of nightingales.

Fingringhoe's Ballast Quay accounts for some of the river's remaining commercial shipping traffic, sending gravel to London and the Channel Isles, mainly in little 200 tonners. The village mill straddles the 'Roman River', which empties into the Colne just below Rowhedge. This end of the Roman River hardly justifies its rather grand and evidently historic name, but it runs for a remarkable distance inland, encircling Colchester to the south and still identifiable beyond the A12 at Marks Tey.

Rowhedge, though nowhere near as pretty as Wivenhoe opposite, is a good place from which to view the river's activity. At its heart is a small town of Victorian brick (and an unusual octagonal church) with a proud history of seafaring and boatbuilding, from smacks to RNLI lifeboats. Conveniently, it has a pub right on the quayside, the Anchor, against which local yachtsmen are welcome to tie up on a midday tide – rather more conveniently, in fact, than motorists trying to find a parking place. Downstream the commercial wharves are now derelict, gradually being swallowed up by modern housing.

Colchester Hythe ... a seafaring history going back to Roman times.

Above the Rowhedge bend the river narrows and straightens for the last couple of miles to Colchester Hythe, closely paralleled by the railway. Travelling on that line to Clacton, I used to contrive to sit on the right side of the train in the hope of seeing a trading coaster negotiating this narrow stretch. There is no longer any chance of that. The swinging area at the Hythe has long been inadequate and has in any case now been cut off beyond a new road bridge. So although Colchester is an ancient port whose seafaring history goes back to Roman times, and the lower quay has been tidied up to berth a collection of barges and fishing vessels in various stages of delapidation – plus a brightly painted ex-Trinity House light vessel used by sea cadets – few other vessels nowadays venture that far.

The view of Wivenhoe's attractive, brightly coloured waterfront that most appeals to photographers and painters is from the opposite bank of the narrow river. But there is no longer a ferry, so the approach is either by train or along the B1028, a turning off the Colchester – Clacton road. This takes you past the University of Essex, whose nearby presence may account for some of the smart new paintwork in the older part of Wivenhoe.

Wivenhoe's attractive and brightly coloured waterfront.

Like Rowhedge, this is basically a Victorian town, built when the local fisheries and shipbuilding were at their peak, with some older weatherboarded or plastered buildings on the quayside, the Rose and Crown in their midst. Some of them combine gardens and mud berths. Nearby you might still see one or two fishing boats.

Quite why Pevsner should have felt that the waterfront has 'no houses of individual interest' I do not understand. One group of white, grandly bay-windowed cottages is simply spectacular; but in any case the overall effect is a delight.

The local sailing club is one of those that maintained a class of wooden, clinker-built one-designs, though the fleet came close to extinction in the 1970s. These 15-footers were designed in the mid-1930s by Dr W. Radcliffe as a slightly larger, tougher version of the West Mersea Sprite.

The traditional craft of wooden boatbuilding is taught a few yards from the club at the Nottage Maritime Institute. Look through the window and you will see that each pupil is building his own superbly finished clinker dinghy.

The Institute goes back to 1896, when wealthy Essex yachtsman Captain Charles Nottage made a bequest to provide sailors with instruction in navigation and seamanship. One of the odd features of the bequest was that there should be no clergymen on the committee!

At various times in its history Wivenhoe engaged in shipbuilding, particularly in the 19th century when it was also famous for its fast yachts. At the outbreak of the Second World War a yard was reopened to build minesweepers and other wooden warships, plus pontoons for the Mulberry harbours that served the Normandy invasion. More recently dredgers, tugs and similar craft were launched from the slipways just below the quay, where a flood barrier has now been constructed. The yard has long since closed, as have the upstream wharves that until quite recently used to unload timber and coal. These are now covered in smart new houses, with many appropriately nautical references in their design, looking across to Rowhedge's empty industrial quayside.

To find somewhere still fully engaged in the modern industrial world, one needs to go a few miles downstream to Brightlingsea. The town's name is derived from the Old English for Bright-ling's 'eye', meaning island. In medieval times it was regarded as an island, and drawn as such on maps – a status the 1953 floods did their best to reassert. Modern sea walls disguise the contours, but if you look at the Ordnance Survey you will see that only a couple of miles of low marshy ground separate the upper reaches of Arlesford and Flag creeks, on either side of the town.

The old church is built on high ground immediately after you cross the head of Arlesford Creek (a rather bleak place, with a derelict ballast quay only accessible until 1964 through a swing railway bridge) on the B1029 road from Thorington. How important the church really was as a navigation mark is difficult to assess in these days of well-lit buoyage and echosounders, but it has been calculated that its 100 foot tower can be seen for 17 miles to seaward, and one of its former vicars, Canon Arthur Pertwee, who took over the parish in 1872, used to climb the tower on stormy nights to place a lantern there.

It was Canon Pertwee who began the unique frieze of commemorative tiles round the church which records all the local sailors who have lost their lives at sea since that time. He was prompted to begin this sad, historically fascinating record by the great equinoctial gale of 6 March, 1883, when three Brightlingsea vessels were lost off the Dutch island of Terschelling, where they had gone in search of oysters. Six men went down with each of them, the smacks *Recruit* and *Conquest*, and the lugger *Mascotte*. The youngest aboard the *Conquest* was aged sixteen – George Parmenter, native of Kirby-le-Soken. Another man was washed overboard and drowned from the smack *Express*.

The big smacks that went deep-sea dredging took their local name of 'skillingers' from the Terschelling grounds. By the end of 1883 another two had been lost with all hands, the *Pride* and the *William and Henry*. In recording these losses, Canon Pertwee decided to go back to the start of his ministry, so the first tiles record the death of David Day and his fifteen year old son, also David, 'lost with his father in the schooner *William* off Hartlepool, Dec. 9, 1872'.

The tradition of the Brightlingsea tiles was continued, using the original stencils. It took a hundred years for them to extend almost right round the church. Sidney Siebert, 'perished in the wreck of the SS *Titanic,* April 15, 1912'; Frank Mills, 'lost from HMS *Queen Mary,* Battle of Jutland, May 31, 1916'; John Sawyer, 'drowned from the barge *Kindly Light* off Southend, July 15, 1925' and so on.

Pertwee's ministry at Brightlingsea was eventful in other ways. In 1884 'the great Essex earthquake', centred just north of here, pitched one of the tower's four pinnacles crashing through the roof of the nave. With his tiles he seemed determined to maintain the links between his medieval church and the prospering Victorian waterside community that had meanwhile grown up at the other end of the island. And symbolically, they still serve that purpose today.

Nobody could accuse Brightlingsea of having tarted itself up. It is a plain, unpretentious little town of brick villas and terraced cottages, the latter mainly laid out in a row of narrow streets leading down to the water. When you emerge on the broad shingle hard you have reached the heart of the place.

At the top of the hard is the solid pile of what was formerly the Anchor Hotel, start and finishing point for a thousand and one boating trips. That role has now been handed on, at least in part, to the nearby Yachtsman's Arms, and the waterside fish-and-chips shop. The latter may not look as if it has much of a history, but step inside and you will see a photograph of this same 'Waterside Café and Oyster Bar' in 1949, standing in several feet of salt water during a spring tidal surge.

To the left as you face the creek is the Colne Yacht Club with its own jetty and pontoon. A famous member, Reg White, was given a hero's welcome back to the town after winning the 1976 Olympic gold medal for Tornado Class catamarans. With a long racing tradition that as professional crew goes back to the great J Class yachts and beyond, local helmsmen have often been at the forefront of technical development, and so it was with the catamaran. Translated from the Pacific atolls to Canvey Island by the Prout brothers in the early 1950s it was enthusiastically developed in Brightlingsea.

Yet at the same time the Colne Yacht Club still shares a thriving fleet of traditional 18 foot Brightlingsea One-Designs with the Brightlingsea Sailing Club in Oyster Tank Road at the lower end of the waterfront. These boats were designed in the 1920s by a local man, Robbie Stone, who also produced designs for the smaller West Mersea Sprites and the Walton Jewels. You will see their bluff-bowed clinker hulls, each painted a distinctive colour, on shallow moorings in the middle of the creek immediately opposite the hard. One or two fishing boats generally bring up in deeper water just downstream – in nothing like the numbers that lay here in the great days of the sprat and oyster fisheries.

On these same moorings today you will probably see one of a new generation of catamarans, quite large working vessels, with a bright orange wheelhouse, that service the offshore wind farm on the Gunfleet Sands. With their double hulls they provide a stable platform from which engineers can transfer to the wind turbine towers – and they are now being built here in the industrial area behind the hard.

Here too is a modern wharf, regularly visited by coasters (though not likely to be flying the Red Ensign) of up to about 4,000 tons. When I last enquired, they were usually loading wood chip to be burnt as fuel in a Swedish power station.

Opposite the mouth of Brightlingsea Creek beyond Bateman's Tower (a recently restored cross between a Victorian folly and a lighthouse) is East Mersea Stone, with the wreck of a ship called the *Lowlands,* and behind that the broad estuary of the Blackwater. In the other direction the channel running inland on the south side of the creek has a narrow branch which leads to the village of St Osyth, with its old barge quay, a boatyard specialising in traditional wooden craft, and a former tidal mill pond.

St Osyth is known locally as 'Toosey' (whereas Brightlingsea is *not* known locally as 'Brittlesea', a yachting writers' myth). The creek has a lot of quiet charm, and pleasant memories for me because I learned to sail there. But the main attraction of the village is its magnificent priory.

The hard at Brightlingsea.

The history of the priory (later an abbey) goes back beyond AD 653, when Osyth was martyred. She was the daughter of Frithwald, first King of the East Angles. Betrothed to the King of Essex, she decided instead to become head of the nunnery. Her martyrdom there was at the hands of two Viking thugs, Inguar and Hubba, who ranged up the creek in their longship looking for plunder. According to medieval religious legend, the Vikings demanded that she renounce her Christianity. When she refused, they cut off her head; whereupon she got up, picked up her severed head and carried it to the door of the church a quarter of a mile away before falling. In the light of this miracle, her relics were believed to possess supernatural power and were certainly profitable. However, a more plausible modern account of her death suggests that the Vikings killed her by cutting her throat, which would explain how she staggered bloodily to the church door before collapsing.

At the seaward end of Colchester's river is Colne Point, with the tiny Ray Creek running in behind its shingle spit. This was always a good place for birdwatching, with cockles and a few reasonably sized mussels below the tideline. As a kid I used to spend hours tramping the beach equipped with a pair of First World War binoculars and a thick ex-army jersey I was convinced kept out the rain. In spring one had to tread carefully to avoid crushing the eggs of the nesting terns and waders, invisible among the pebbles; in winter snow buntings would drift in on the east wind, while grebes, divers and mergansers found shelter behind the point. Sailing barges loaded ballast at the quay.

Now, appropriately enough, the whole area is a reserve managed by the Essex Wildlife Trust and approached by road from St Osyth, through Leewick Farm (visitors are warned that the little car park may be covered at spring tides). Among the many specialised plants that have found a place for themselves in the shingle are sea holly and the yellow horned poppy.

From Colne Point, the coast runs northeast in a smooth, twelve mile curve to the Naze. The shoreline is punctuated by Martello towers and Second World War blockhouses, reminders that this was reckoned a likely invasion point for Napoleon's armies as well as Hitler's. Seaside resorts at Clacton and Walton stand on low cliffs, separated by the choked-off inlet of the old Holland Haven, and each has its pier, lifeboat station and amusement arcades.

This is also one of the East Anglian shores from which you can most closely view the offshore wind farms proliferating across the Thames Estuary and the Wash, annoying the fishermen but providing welcome jobs for coastal communities. In this case four dozen of those slender turbines stand hundreds of feet tall on the Gunfleet Sands; a ghostly forest, turned to face the wind.

Fossil hunting on Naze Ledge.

WALTON BACKWATERS

WALTON-ON-THE-NAZE – KIRBY-LE-SOKEN – BEAUMONT-CUM-MOZE

A STRANGER VISITING Walton by road should drive straight up on to the Naze, park alongside the great octagonal seamark standing there, and take in the local geography.

The Naze (or Nose) was a place in its own right before the ancient village of Walton-le-Soken expanded onto it to form the present seaside resort. It is a promontory of crumbling red crag underlain by clay, with a covering of rough grass and gorse bushes. To the north you can walk on a looping footpath out to Walton Stone, the shingle spit which forms the base of the Pye Sand. Behind that the muddy backwaters creep round to the west until they almost reach the sea again, and turn Walton into an island.

To seaward of the tower (where in summer you can buy a cup of tea or visit the art gallery on an upper floor) you will find notices warning of dangerous cliff falls, as the land is constantly being eroded. When the tower was built in 1720 it was 500 yards from the cliff edge; on my last visit that distance had diminished to little more than 50 yards, though it is hoped that the stone-built 'crag path' recently constructed on the beach below will slow things down. Miles away to the northeast, the underwater bank known as the West Rocks was probably once part of the Naze, forming the southern arm of Harwich harbour entrance.

The newly exposed cliffs are a great place for fossils: primaeval bird skeletons, crabs and shark teeth in the 50 million-year-old clay; and the famous 'reversed whelk' which spirals the opposite way to its modern cousins, in the much younger red crag. It is also said that in the Ice Age some of the last herds of woolly mammoths took refuge on this high ground from the encroaching glaciers.

It was certainly the unusual height of the Naze, by East Anglian standards, that persuaded Trinity House to build the brown brick, 80-foot Naze Tower in 1720. This is one seamark that must really have earned its keep before coastal buoyage became so prolific. From out at sea it is visible when the rest of the coast is just a misty blur, serving to guide vessels through Goldmer Gat, north of the Gunfleet Sand immediately opposite the Naze.

Closer inshore, marking one of the shallower approach channels to Harwich across the bay and bearing about ESE from the tower, you should be able to make out the Medusa buoy. This has an authentic tale to tell. It was named after Nelson's frigate of 1801, trapped in Harwich because she could not beat out against the wind through the normal deep-water channel to the northeast. Nelson was impatient to be away; some say because he feared the French might land in Suffolk, some because he was tired of visiting his wife in Ipswich. At any rate he made his impatience known and a local hydrographer, Graeme Spence, offered to pilot the clumsy warship, drawing 16 feet, out through this alternative route.

If you do walk out beyond the Naze, bear in mind that part of this area has been set aside as a reserve for birds, plants and insects. During the early summer 'bird tides', the somewhat lower tides that allow sea birds to nest safely on the shoreline, the Essex Wildlife Trust does its best to protect little terns and other species which breed along here. Near the reserve, incidentally, several human skeletons have been unearthed on the site of an early Iron Age settlement.

If you know what you are looking for, blackish 'copperas stones' can be collected along this beach, as they were for several centuries. They were a source of ferrous sulphate for use in the tanning, dyeing and ink-making industries.

Modern Walton is a product of the Victorian craze for sea bathing and the relatively early arrival of the railway from London, in 1867. The name of the Bath House Hotel recalls those early days when visitors either took to the health-giving waters in the privacy of their bathroom or ventured out into the new 'bathing machines' on the beach. The first large hotel, the Portobello, began the major seafront development in 1829. A small jetty was erected a year later (the same date as the start of Southend Pier), followed by the present pier in 1869 as the coastal paddle steamers began to need deeper water.

Any paddle steamer trying to range alongside Walton Pier these days would risk coming foul of moored 'crawly' nets, crab and lobster pots, marked by little black-flagged dan buoys bobbing and swirling in the tide. There seem to be more of them every time I sail past. In summer they are worked either off the beach from fast open boats, or round from Walton Channel. The traditional Essex hoop net, incidentally, baited with flounder or whelks, has apparently given way to framed netting pots, with one-way entrances and separate 'lobster parlours' to prevent the trapped creatures attacking one another.

The long pier still performs an important seafaring function by providing an afloat mooring for the Walton and Frinton lifeboat (one of two institutions incidentally, where downmarket Walton takes rightful precedence over posh Frinton; the other being the Walton and Frinton Yacht Club). There has been an RNLI lifeboat on this station since 1884, the original one bought with funds raised at drama club 'smoking concerts' arranged by the Honourable Artillery Company. For the next 30 years or so there was intense rivalry between the RNLI boat and a private lifeboat, the *True to the Core*, run by local watermen. Perhaps this was because rescues held out the prospect of lucrative salvage as well as the hope of saving lives. At any rate it was to match this rival that the RNLI provided Walton with a bigger boat in 1900, to lie afloat off the pier (and since 2005 right alongside it) instead of launching across the beach. The old lifeboat house on East Terrace (itself a splendid example of Victorian speculative building) has been refurbished by the Frinton and Walton Heritage Trust and is now maintained as a maritime museum. Its weathered brick and tile makes a nice contrast with the Coastguard station alongside, festooned with the aerials of modern maritime technology – though not for much longer, since the station is threatened with closure in 2014.

Walton remains an amiable seafront resort of the traditional buckets and spades variety. But dive down Mill Lane off the High Street and you look out – albeit through a forest of yacht masts – on to an entirely different environment of creeks and mud, sea walls, brambles and blackthorn. The creeks forming the backwaters reach inland for several miles in every direction until they come up against a sea wall or a sluice. The main channel, Hamford Water, is quite deep once you cross the bar, and coasters use it to serve the explosives factory on Bramble Island. The creeks which penetrate deep into the fields at Kirby and Beaumont end in tiny, derelict quays that were used within living memory by great brown-sailed sailing barges trading to the farms. They even had their own local pilots, known as 'hufflers'.

Walton Channel, immediately behind the Naze, provides deep, clear water for moorings, petering out in the town's muddy creek. In 1922 the Walton and Frinton Yacht Club built its present clubhouse there, on the foundations of an old windmill (the club's tower was an anti-submarine lookout moved from the town seafront). Curiously, there had

The thatched cottage at Kirby Quay.

been another mill alongside, worked by the tides, whose catchment pool later made a fine boating lake for the kids. Like other Essex clubs, Walton used to have its own 18-foot clinker one-design. That gave way to the 14 foot Jewel class, a small fleet of which (mainly wooden) are still raced, though you would search hard now to find them among their ubiquitous successors. At the time of writing, the club is about to embark on a major rebuild.

Below Foundry Reach, which served Walton's Foundry Dock as well as the two mills, the permanent deep water turns west into the Twizzle. The shingle landing there, Colonel's Hard, has long been superseded by the marina the Titchmarsh family dug out from behind the sea wall. Upstream I believe there are still oyster layings, as there are in Kirby Creek on the other side of Horsey Island.

Horsey is the main island of the archipelago. According to *The Place-names of Essex,* its meaning is obvious: Hors-ey, or 'horse-island' (and it has in fact been used in modern times for breeding horses). Anyone old and square enough to have been brought up on Arthur Ransome will remember Horsey and the backwaters as the setting for one of his most delightful books, *Secret Water.* As with most of his writing for children, every geographical detail was accurate and described with great clarity. Most remarkably, hardly anything has changed.

The low-tide shingle causeway to Horsey, known as 'the Wade', is one of several places where one can reach the water from a road skirting the backwaters to the south – though nowadays only by foot. From the concrete wartime pillbox at the end of the causeway a public footpath leads westward along the sea wall to the old barge quay at the head of Kirby Creek, with its tarred pilot cottage (not the prettier thatched one, which looks more the part). The house raised on piles immediately adjacent to the quay was built round the structure of the old granary.

I mention this footpath particularly, because although some of these lanes are worth poking down, not all the local landowners accept the traditional public usage of sea walls. It seems the argument goes back to the days when each farmer maintained his stretch of wall – inadequately as it turned out. In law, a sea wall is not by definition a right of way, though in my view it certainly should be.

Farther west another lane (also with no public access for cars) leads down to Landermere, a pretty little beach where a few boats usually lie. Beyond that again, a mile or so from Thorpe-le-Soken (the third of the ancient local communities to be granted 'soken', or rights to manage their own affairs) the backwaters penetrate to their furthest inland point. Just before the B1414 road turns back towards Harwich, a tiny scattered village has the imposing name of Beaumont-cum-Moze (the 'fair hill' beside the 'marshy place'). A short lane leads down to a farm where a public footpath takes you a few yards round to the stone-faced Beaumont Quay (with its own wooden sign and small car park).

Nowhere could you find a more unlikely, more thoroughly agricultural setting for a seagoing vessel than this. Yet the flat-bottomed Thames sailing barges regularly traded to such apparently inaccessible spots, brown topsails moving slowly across the flat skyline. Beaumont was actually 'home port' to a couple of barges, the *Beaumont Belle* and the little *Gleaner,* 28 tons, built especially to negotiate the cut leading up to the quay (though an overhead power cable would now prevent this). They carried grain, timber, coal, fertilisers, bricks, road-making materials – almost anything the farming communities wanted to shift. The *Gleaner's* name hints at the most remarkable trade of all, summed up in the phrase 'hay out, muck in'. 'Stackies' sailed from creeks like this with a haystack lashed down on deck, bound for London and its horses; the barges would reload with manure and bring it back to the farms – a perfect trading symmetry.

You can visualise all this by walking down through the long grass to Beaumont Quay, where one of the old warehouses still stands. A stone inscription that formerly told their remarkable story seems to have disappeared, but I can tell you what it said:

> This building and quay
> was erected by the
> Governors of Guys Hospital
> 1832
> —Harrison Esq. Treasurer
> The stone used in the quay formed part
> of London Bridge built about
> 1176

Walton Backwaters.

On the saltings above the quay a broken-backed barge was left to rot. She was a stackie, the *Rose,* from Maldon, where as it happened, the *Beaumont Belle* ended her days on the mud beside the old timber wharf.

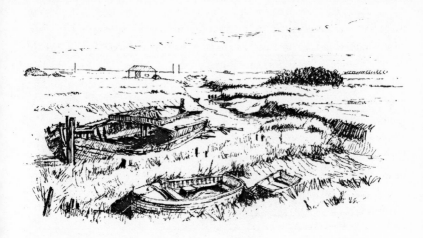

A lingering death for the sailing barge Rose *at Beaumont Quay.*

The wheel crane at Harwich.

HARWICH HARBOUR AND THE RIVER STOUR

HARWICH – ERWARTON – HOLBROOK – WRABNESS – MISTLEY –
MANNINGTREE – FLATFORD

HARWICH HARBOUR shelters two separate ports: Harwich itself, which has the history, and the vast modern port of Felixstowe, a product of the shipping industry's 'container revolution.'

The town of Harwich stands at the mouth of the Stour, a broad, placid, beautiful river largely neglected by yachtsmen. Whereas yachts by the hundred crowd moorings on the neighbouring River Orwell, few penetrate the Stour beyond the busy ferry terminals of Parkeston Quay. Those that do can find quiet anchorages and reasonably hard landing at Erwarton Ness and Wrabness cliff (albeit without the amenity of a nearby pub or restaurant), and beyond that a winding channel to the small upriver port of Mistley.

As you drive into Harwich the public quay is at the far end of the town, with a few parking slots by the waterside, and it is only a short walk from the railway station. The quay overlooks 'the Pound' where local fishing boats traditionally lie. On your right as you face the water is Ha'penny Pier, from which a passenger ferry runs in summer to Shotley and Landguard Point. To your left is the Trinity House pier, easily identified by the brightly painted navigational buoys stacked alongside like giant spinning tops, and in the distance beyond that is Parkeston Quay, the ferry terminal for Holland and Scandinavia as well as a shore base for several offshore wind farms.

Across the river is Shotley, and its yacht marina. The village developed there round the naval training establishment HMS *Ganges*. That closed a long time ago, but for generations of young sailors its forbidding grey roofs and white, square-rigged mast were their first glimpse of the Royal Navy.

Battleship grey has now given way to Trinity House red, the high-visibility colour used for light vessels. A privately owned example of these engineless floating lighthouses is permanently moored at

The buoys are back in town . . . Trinity House Pier, Harwich.

Harwich Quay and Trinity House itself keeps a spare vessel alongside its pier.

The 'Trinity House Lighthouse Service', to give it its proper name and distinguish it from the associated pilotage service, has one of its two main depots at Harwich. Lighthouses, light vessels and navigational buoys right round the English coastline are controlled from there, and those on the eastern side of the country directly maintained.

As you would imagine, respect for traditional methods runs pretty deep in an organisation that traces its history back six hundred years to a charter from Henry VIII, but wherever modern technology proves capable of surviving in a rigorous salt water environment, it has taken over. The light buoys peering above the wall of the maintenance yard at Harwich (30 feet high some of them) are powered by solar panels, not the old acetylene gas, and the actual lanterns are mainly low-energy LEDs, sending out a coded pattern of white, red or green flashes to show mariners where the channel runs or the hazard lies. Buoys are normally left on station for several years, although individual components can if necessary be changed at sea. Eventually the whole unit is retrieved by one of the Trinity House tenders, complete with heavy mooring chain and cast iron sinker, and dumped on the Harwich pier for cleaning and repainting.

One modern development that did *not* catch on is the LANBY (large automatic navigational buoy), partly for the curious reason that no engineer (one of them assured me of this) has ever been able to work down below in its circular, 40-foot wide hull without becoming seasick. The only LANBY I encountered at sea also displayed a notice warning that its foghorn was dangerously loud. (Which surely means that by the time you can read the warning, it will be too late?)

In the days when light vessels were manned – by a master and four 'lightsmen' working a 28-day shift – I'm told the crew were paid extra while the foghorn was sounding, rather like the Royal Navy's 'hard lying' money. Now everything is automated. The last lighthouse to be converted, on the North Foreland, went automatic in 1998.

Where light vessels are concerned, I suppose yachtsmen generally regretted the change while having no inclination to do such a monotonous job themselves. Encountering a light vessel at sea still brings the reassurance of a known position – a feeling inversely proportional to one's navigational skill. Knowing there was a human being aboard, who kept a lookout and would probably give a friendly wave as you passed, added greatly to that reassurance.

One of the early Masters of Trinity House was the diarist Samuel Pepys, who became Secretary to the Admiralty and later MP for Harwich. The unique wooden treadmill crane which has been preserved and re-erected on the grass behind the town quay was already standing on the site of the present Navyard Wharf when he arrived in 1674 to organise repairs to the storm damaged naval shipyard. Harwich had proved its worth as a naval base during the wars with Holland. But the connection goes back to 885, when King Alfred's Saxon fleet took on the Danes at the battle of 'Stourmouth', and in our own times the navy returned in force during two world wars.

Fishing has never been quite the major industry one might expect in such a convenient port. The 18th and 19th century 'cod bangers' (because cod kept alive in the smack's flooded well were killed with a club just before landing) represented a long tradition of deep-sea line fishing as far afield as Iceland; by the end of the 19th century Harwich bawleys were busy trawling and boiling pink shrimps, and they took their share of the local lobsters. Yet somehow the Harwich men never made their fisheries pay on the large industrial scale of Lowestoft or Yarmouth.

One key to any fishing port's commercial development was a railway link to Billingsgate. But when the railway was finally extended to Harwich quay from Manningtree it was seen as an opportunity to expand a different form of seafaring – passenger services to the Continent, which had also been part of the local scene since medieval times.

Mail packets began sailing from Harwich in 1661 to the little fortified harbour of Hellevoetsluis, south of Rotterdam, which now sits pretty and protected behind a great estuarial dam. The packet boats also carried passengers, among them on one occasion another great diarist, James Boswell. He took passage aboard the *Prince of Wales* in

1763, and described how Dr Johnson came down to Harwich quay to see the ship off.

In 1836, however, the mail contract was lost to Dover; Harwich captains were reluctant to switch from sail to steam. Six years later the opening of the big new Ipswich dock upriver was another blow. Harwich was in decline and looking desperately for a railway-based passenger service to revive its economic fortunes. After several attempts the railway did arrive in 1854. Nine years later the Great Eastern Railway obtained Parliamentary permission to build its 'Continental Pier' at the western end of the waterfront (now the Trinity House pier) and inaugurate connecting ferry services to Rotterdam.

Old Harwich seemed after all to have found a place in the modern commercial world of iron and steam. As if in celebration, a spendidly imposing railway hotel was built right on the quayside. It is still there, an ornate building in faded yellow brick and stone that served for a while as the town hall. Its original promise, however, was never fulfilled. Harwich Corporation turned out to have neither the business acumen nor the physical space on its short waterfront to capitalise on the railway's arrival. The Great Eastern Railway was soon using bigger steamers of over 1,000 tons, for which it wanted more quay space and plentiful supplies of water. Harwich was unable or unwilling to provide either. In 1874 the GER lost patience and decided to build its own deep-water terminal across the bay on what was then the Isle of Ray, outside the Corporation's jurisdiction.

It was a vast engineering scheme (described in detail in Wilfred Wren's *Ports of the Eastern Counties*). Several hundred acres were reclaimed to join the island to the mainland and provide room for the new railway workers' estate of Parkeston, named after the GER chairman Charles Parkes. As a final snub to Harwich, a new railway hotel was built alongside his quay.

It is a story of neighbouring rivalry that has been repeated in several other places along the East Coast. Harwich lost out, but one gets the feeling that this stubbornly independent community would not spend too much time crying into its beer.

Eventually, in 1924, the town did manage to make something of its original link with the railway (by then the LNER), which brought a secondhand train ferry terminal round from Southampton, reassembled it alongside Gas House Creek and opened a service to Zeebrugge that continued into the 1980s. This venture was followed in 1964 by redevelopment of the Navyard at the opposite, eastern corner of the waterfront, providing roll-on roll-off services to Germany, Scandinavia and Russia.

That, for the moment, is more or less the extent of the town's commercial development, though there are ambitious plans to build a new container port on the adjacent Bathside mudflats. Harwich is a town for sailors, not shipowners. The lifeboat and the pilot cutters are based here, as well as Trinity House. While most of the ships berth at neighbouring Parkeston or Felixstowe, they are controlled from a modern radar operations room just round the corner from the town quay, overlooking the harbour entrance. Sharing the view are some of the few distinguished looking houses in Harwich, two of them with elegant bow windows stacked one above the other. I have always fantasised that they were built for retired sea captains who sat over their gin, keeping a critical eye on the ships as they came and went.

One of the town's most famous captains, Christopher Jones, lived more modestly nearby at number 21, Kings Head Street, one of the narrow streets running straight back from the quay. The Pilgrim Fathers may have taken their final departure from Plymouth, but it was from Harwich that the *Mayflower* originally set sail, commanded by Jones, in July 1620. His passengers mostly embarked at Southampton, and in November of that year he landed them in New England. Jones was twice married in the church of St Nicholas, which marks the Harwich skyline from seaward. The brick building you see now, with its display of Dutch tiles, was rebuilt in 1822, when its slender cast iron pillars were the latest thing. But a church was first built there in 1177 and by the early 18th century it must already have acquired a tall spire because one sees it in contemporary pictures, looking much as it does today.

Just opposite, according to one of the Harwich Society's highly informative plaques, stands probably the oldest house in Harwich, a former alehouse dating from the 15th century and known locally as 'the old drum and monkey'. Harwich always seems to have been well supplied with pubs, as befits a seafaring town, and this remains true. It also has one or two restaurants, and the splendidly restored 'Electric Palace' cinema that first opened in 1911.

Not far from the church, opposite where the medieval town gate stood, the houses give way to a simple grass promenade, with the Harwich Town Yacht Club and a lifeboat museum at one end (the Royal Harwich Yacht Club is upriver at Woolverstone) and the stone breakwater which partially closes the harbour entrance at the other. Here you can see the treadmill crane mentioned earlier, believed to be the only one of its kind, and two old lighthouses, the High and Low Lights, with canopied roofs like a pair of salt and pepper pots. They were erected as leading lights to guide ships into the harbour from the northeast, but by the middle of the century they had become known as the 'misleading lights', symptoms of a piece of misguided local enterprise that nearly ruined this great natural haven.

Hard setting clay or 'septaria' from the Beacon Cliff forming the western side of Harwich harbour entrance had long been used

Harwich high and low lights for shipping.

locally as a building material. Defoe refers to it at some length in his 18th century *Tour:*

'The account of a petrifying quality in the earth here, tho' some will have it to be in the water of a spring hard by, is very strange: They boast that their town is wall'd, and their streets pav'd with clay, and yet, that one is as strong, and the other as clean as those that are built or pav'd with stone.'

This same clay was also known as Roman cement stone, because it could be burnt in a kiln and used as cement, and it was this second usage that was nearly the undoing of Harwich.

In 1808 the cement was used in the construction of a circular fortress, the Redoubt, overlooking the harbour entrance from behind the Beacon Cliff. It was to match the older fortress on Landguard Point opposite, and part of an extensive programme of coastal defences against Napoleonic invasion that included the Martello towers. Restored by the indefatigable Harwich Society, it is well worth a visit, and if you or your children enjoy poking around such things there are also plenty of bramble covered Second World War gun emplacements on the point nearby.

After the Napoleonic wars the local cement industry flourished, rapidly excavating the Beacon Cliff for its raw material. Still more clay was dredged from the Felixstowe side of the harbour. As the shape of the entrance changed it began to silt up, presumably because there was less tidal scour. Landguard Point began to extend across the channel in alarming fashion, just as Orfordness had done further north. The Admiralty in particular feared that it was about to lose a major strategic asset, a natural deep-water harbour that Defoe recalled sheltering 'a hundred sail of men-of-war and their attendants, and between three and four hundred sail of collier ships, all in this harbour at a time'.

The first remedial move was to forbid digging away the cliffs, although the special 'aquatic cement' that would set under water was still in demand. Then they built a breakwater as an artificial substitute for the Beacon Cliff. But it took a second groyne on the Felixstowe side to redirect the flow so as to erode the shingle spit that had grown out from Landguard. The harbour was saved, though evidently it never quite recovered its original form.

If you climb the pretty iron balustraded stairs to the 'front door' of the taller lighthouse on the green and look out across the Low Light, you will see that a line between them would nowadays lead ships straight on to Landguard Point. They were built in 1818 to replace an earlier pair, one of which stood on the town gate behind the High Light and the other down on the beach. If the French fleet were sighted during the Napoleonic wars, the plan was to blow up the lower leading light and replace it – in the wrong position – by a replica that was kept in the Guildhall in Church Street.

The Dovercourt lights ... unlit monuments to local maritime history.

Thanks to the success of the cement industry, the beautiful new stock-brick lighthouses were soon misleading. In 1863 they were therefore shut down, though fortunately not demolished (the lower one has become a museum), and replaced as leading lights by two iron pile structures on Dovercourt beach. Those in their turn were eventually abandoned, before being renovated in 1975 as unlit monuments to local maritime history. Dovercourt had meanwhile bloomed and faded as a seaside resort, complete with streets of bay-windowed villas, a Marine Parade, and a statue of Queen Victoria.

Above Parkeston, the River Stour's main channel holds to the northern bank, opposite the mudflats of Copperas Bay (named after the ferrous sulphate nodules or 'copperas stones' that used to be collected off Harwich for dyeing and tanning). Erwarton Ness, with the remains of an old barge quay that once served the local farms, is a favourite anchorage for yachtsmen – or at any rate was so until the village pub closed. Notwithstanding this loss, Erwarton and its church, a flinted building with broad Perpendicular windows looking out over the river, have a remarkable story from Tudor times.

It seems that Henry VIII's wife Anne Boleyn often visited her uncle at nearby Erwarton Hall (you can't miss its extravagent turreted gatehouse), and when the King ordered her execution she asked that her heart be buried in the village church. When the building was refurbished in the early 19th century a heart-shaped casket was indeed found in an alcove, containing a dark powder assumed to be her pathetic remains. They were reburied beneath the organ.

A couple of miles further upstream is Holbrook Creek, with a shallow anchorage near the beacon at its entrance. Landward access is by footpath from a car park on the Lower Holbrook road – good walking and birdwatching country. The fine reed beds here, incidentally, are cut for thatching.

At this point the main river channel swings across to the southern bank to scour close under the sandy cliffs of Wrabness. The village has

Wrecked at Wrabness.

its own railway station, a church with a free-standing wooden belfry, and a few scattered houses. Its main asset is a pretty little beach that offers deep-water moorings and a rare chance in this part of the world to swim at half-tide without wading through mud. You can leave a car near the church and walk down a private road that leads to some beach huts. The impressive building with the tall pointed tower on the far side of the river is Holbrook School, which has close ties with the Royal Navy. At the bottom of the lane turn left for the beach, or you can take the sea wall footpath to the right, along the edge of Copperas Bay and back up through the trees. This extremely ancient woodland is jointly managed by the Essex Wildlife Trust, the RSPB and the Woodland Trust, and can also be reached from the Mistley–Harwich road. Its hornbeams and sweet chestnuts – some of which are said to have been there since Roman times – are once more being coppiced in traditional fashion.

A further three miles upstream the channel again swings hard against the southern bank of the river, enabling quite large coasting vessels to reach the quays of Mistley, and then winds more uncertainly the last mile or so to Manningtree. This is the first crossing point for road and rail, and formerly the place at which the tidal Stour briefly overlapped the canalised Stour Navigation.

Manningtree lays claim to have been the smallest town in England because its parish comprises only 22 acres. It also had the unfortunate distinction of providing the first batch of seven victims for the 17th century witch hunter Matthew Hopkins, who set up business at The White Hart.

Hopkins was paid twenty shillings per witch by Parliament. Having enlisted the help of a local 'searcher', his technique was to find some old lady against whom the neighbours had a grudge, then bully her into admitting something that would justify putting her to the witch test. This was of the 'heads I win, tails you lose' variety. Having tied her hands and feet together, the victim was 'swum'; if she sank she was innocent, if she floated she was guilty and hanged.

Manningtree is a much more cheerful place these days. Like its neighbour Mistley, the town's early prosperity was connected with ships and maltings. It has some extremely elegant houses and a tiny waterfront and quay that come briefly alive as the last of the flood tide brims up over the mud. The Stour Sailing Club, whose dinghies launch across the narrow beach, is exceptional in sponsoring a small fleet of racing gun punts.

Some notable wildfowling families once worked this river, where I am told there was a tradition of 'fast punts and small guns'. Punts have always set a small spritsail or some other scrap of canvas to fetch back and forth to their gunners' favourite creeks, and they would sometimes turn out for the local regatta along with other working craft. At Manningtree they have come to be raced for their own sake. But whereas in Norfolk this led to the evolution of a highly specialised boat that lost sight of its original purpose, here on the Stour they still compete in simple square-sectioned craft steered with an oar.

Walk back to Mistley along 'the walls' and almost certainly the first thing to catch your eye will be a group of swans, smoothly stemming the tide or plodding ungainly through the mud by Hopping Bridge. I have always associated Mistley with swans, assuming them to be attracted by the maltings that have been an important local industry since at least the 17th century. Supporting evidence that the association goes back a long way is the swan-shaped fountain, neglected but still magnificent, that stands in the small square by the quay. The water splashing from the swan's beak is piped from a hillside spring behind the Thorn Hotel opposite. The oval basin that collects it was to have been the cold water supply for an ambitious 18th century scheme to build a 'saltwater bath' on the quay behind the fountain, and turn Mistley into a fashionable spa.

The man behind the scheme was the scandalous Richard Rigby of Mistley Hall, Member of Parliament and military Paymaster General to George III. His father had made money by speculating in the South Sea Bubble; the son did equally well from equally dubious activities that included the lucrative army boot contract. And he was also evidently a man of great social ambition, who numbered the Adam brothers among his smart friends. It was Robert Adam who designed Rigby's

The swan fountain at Mistley.

bath house or 'bagno' in 1774. It would have supplanted the little row of houses with a semicircular porch, and the building alongside which now houses a craft workshop, all of which seem to have been part of the original quayside maltings and granary. In fact the scheme was never carried through, but Robert Adam did begin work two years later on spectacular embellishments of the small brick church at the northwest end of the quay.

Adam's plan was to buttress the existing nave with two square towers decorated by Tuscan-style columns. It was his only venture into ecclesiastical architecture and survives today as little more than a curiosity. In *The Buildings of England,* Nikolaus Pevsner dismisses the design as daring but aesthetically not wholly successful. Without even the intervening nave, demolished when the Victorian church was built up the road, the empty towers seem particularly cheerless. And since meeting Ivan Garwood, an authority on local history who for many years ran the maltings there, I cannot help remembering the grim story of the 'Mistley Hound'. It seems that when they built the church, a dog was buried alive alongside it 'to ward off ghouls'. Since then the riverside walls between Mistley and Manningtree have been haunted by the wretched animal's ghost. Mr Garwood admits to having seen it himself.

Robert Adam's only venture into ecclesiastical architecture . . . at Mistley.

The Rigby estates were sold up in 1844. Forty years later Mistley Hall was demolished, though the two lodges Robert Adam built for it can still be seen up the hill at the junction of the Clacton and Colchester roads. But this pleasant little town continues to earn its living in much the same way, making malt for the breweries and handling small ships of up to about 3,000 tons at its quay – bringing cargoes like bricks, metals or coal in, and grain or malt out. The fountain still works, though no-one needs its water. I gather it was a condition of the Rigby sale that the supply should be maintained – as it has been – from a spring on the hill.

The ancient art of malting – spreading out barley to germinate and become 'green malt' that can be used to produce brewing sugar – is now a highly mechanised, scientific process. At Mistley the business moved up the hill many years ago, leaving the quay to be redeveloped. However, this has recently prompted fierce argument (unresolved at the time of writing) over public access. Whereas the eastern end of the quay is obviously a commercial operation, the western end, by a group of cottages facing the water, has always been regarded by local and visiting yachtsmen as a public quay – indeed there is nowhere else for them to tie up. But this section has currently been rendered unusable as a mooring place by the erection of a two-metre-high steel fence.

The small shipyard downstream has a significant history. The 32-gun frigate HMS *Amphion*, briefly Nelson's flagship, was launched from there in 1798. More recently it was the home of the Horlock fleet of sailing barges, one of the most famous on the East Coast. The Horlocks were farmers who took to barging in the 19th century and were among the last to succumb to the competition of diesel power and road transport. Many of the barges that have survived as yachts were owned or built at Mistley, including *Marjorie*, and the steel-hulled *Repertor*, *Reminder* and *Xylonite* (a reference to the old name of the plastics factory just upriver on the other bank, where, incidentally, Margaret Thatcher worked as a young woman).

Part of the Mistley sailing barges' work was to tranship grain into lighters or canal barges that would take it up to inland mills on the Stour Navigation and return with flour. The 40-foot canal boats might set a makeshift squaresail to help them across the mile or two of tidal water to the Cattawade lock. From there they were

The quay at Mistley.

towed in pairs by horses. One of my uncles' boyhood tales was of the horses jumping aboard to shoot Stratford St Mary bridge. These same barges have become familiar to a vast audience from John Constable's paintings.

The Stour was canalised in 1713, with fifteen locks from Cattawade to Sudbury, Gainsborough's birthplace. As with many of these coastal navigations, coal was an important early cargo. Later it was the mills that provided the work, with the last freight carried to Dedham in 1928. John Constable's father owned a barge-building yard just upstream from Flatford Mill, now owned and superbly presented by the National Trust. The double-ended boats were planked up in a little dock at right angles to the bank, that could be emptied through a wooden culvert under the river.

Art historians worked out some time ago that the site of the dock shown in Constable's painting 'Boat building' (now in the Victoria and Albert museum) must be the tiny inlet, with a bridge over it, alongside the café at Flatford. In 1985 the flooded dock was drained and revealed the remains of a barge, dramatically confirming what academics had already deduced from the fact that Constable painted this particular scene on the spot – an unusual thing for those days. The barge was painstakingly reconstructed and is now used to take tourists on trips up the river – a reminder that this quiet, landlocked stream was once a busy commercial waterway, giving access to the wider world of salt water and the North Sea.

8

FELIXSTOWE AND THE RIVER ORWELL

FELIXSTOWE – LEVINGTON – IPSWICH – WOOLVERSTONE – PIN MILL

FOR SEVERAL HUNDRED years the Harwich Harbour skyline could be identified from seaward by the slender spire of its parish church. After the Second World War, when I first started to sail in there, a more useful landmark was the big hammerhead crane on the Felixstowe shore opposite, associated with the seaplane base rather than the tiny railway dock nearby. Now the scene is dominated by Felixstowe, where a long row of long-legged gantry cranes serves what by 1984 could claim to be the biggest container port in the United Kingdom.

Felixstowe is the East Coast's commercial success story, an example of 20th century enterprise to match the Victorian development of Parkeston Quay or Lowestoft. Defoe would have been particularly pleased to see an East Anglian port hitting back at London, which in his day was already beginning to 'suck the vitals' of its coastal neighbours – the victim he had mainly in mind being Ipswich, at the head of the River Orwell.

Felixstowe's history as a port goes back no more than a hundred years. Before that there was a nearby village, Old Felixstowe, which must have had links both with the waterside community at the entrance to the River Deben and with the military fortress standing on Landguard Point to guard the northern arm of Harwich Harbour.

This great natural haven, formerly known as Orwell Haven, is believed to have been fortified even in Roman times, when the Felixstowe cliffs and the Naze both extended a couple of miles further to seaward and both carried the name Walton (still remembered as a district of Felixstowe). The original Landguard fort was built in 1626, on the shingle spit which by then had begun to stretch south across the old harbour entrance, and it was only abandoned by the British Army in 1956. It was designed by a Dutchman, yet found its place in military history by defending Harwich against a Dutch invasion in 1667, during the closing stages of the second Anglo-Dutch war.

The Dutch fleet commanded by de Ruyter was cock-a-hoop after a successful raid on the Medway, where it had burned several English warships and captured the flagship *Royal Charles*. Now the Dutch Admiral sailed past Harwich to Orfordness, luring the panicking Suffolk militia across the Deben ferry in pursuit, then swept back on Landguard.

De Ruyter's plan was to send two squadrons in to bombard the fort from either side of Landguard Point, while a landing party attacked it from the Felixstowe side. But in spite of his personal efforts to organise this elaborate strategy, rowing furiously between the ships, it soon began to fall apart. One Dutch squadron found that the Platters shoal was shallower than it thought (I know the feeling) while the other was becalmed in the harbour entrance. Instead, a small group of English ships managed to work across to the western side of Landguard to bombard the Dutch infantry exposed on the shingle. The militia had meanwhile struggled back across the Deben and came down the cliffs to drive the invaders back to their boats. Harwich was saved.

The Landguard fort was rebuilt in the 18th and 19th centuries, with additions during two world wars – a dark sprawling complex, part restored and open to the public thanks to the enthusiasm of Felixstowe's historical society, part derelict, its blind gun emplacements staring useless across the harbour entrance. But if you want to watch one of the vast container ships negotiating that tight bend in the entrance channel, or perhaps migrating birds taking a rest on Landguard Common, this is the place to go. A foot ferry across the harbour also runs from there in summer.

The Victorian port of Felixstowe was created, as were many others, in partnership with the railway. It was the work of an eccentric local landowner, Colonel Tomline, who formed the Felixstowe Dock & Railway Company in 1879. He dreamed of a great new port to rival Harwich and Ipswich, coupled with a fashionable seaside resort that would be served by the same railway. It did not work out in his time, but he did bring the railway, and until recently, the tidal basin he excavated at the mouth of the old Walton Creek remained at the centre of the modern port, the old wooden dock office and former Pier Hotel reminding one how it began. During the Second World War, this small dock became a base for air-sea rescue launches and torpedo boats. It was here, when the war was over, that the Royal Navy accepted the surrender of the German E-boat squadrons. The dock was finally filled in to provide two new deep-water berths for the next generation of ultra large container ships, each capable of carrying 18,000 containers.

Felixstowe's explosive growth as a commercial port began in the 1950s, when the Norfolk grain merchant Gordon Parker acquired the company. Undeterred by the 1953 flood, which almost wiped out the original port facilities, his management took advantage of the destruction to improve them. Next came a deep-water oil terminal and then one expansion scheme after another, unhindered by the dock labour disputes which afflicted London's outmoded managerial and manning structure. Above all, Felixstowe became an enthusiastic part of the 'container revolution', the new form of general cargo handling to which London only adapted by abandoning its up-river docks for Tilbury.

The River Orwell... a peaceful and yet busy navigation.

Above Felixstowe, the River Orwell leaves Harwich Harbour in a northerly direction and then turns round Collimer Point into Long Reach and Butterman's Bay. The last name recalls the fast schooners that were built on this coast to carry perishable cargoes; it was also the reach where large steamships would moor to be offloaded into barges or lighters when the Orwell was less vigorously dredged than it is today.

The only obvious access to the river's northeast shore between Felixstowe and Ipswich is at Levington, approached by road from various turnings off the A45. If you enjoy browsing among boats make for the Suffolk Yacht Harbour, a highly convenient artificial marina for visiting yachtsmen, cut into the bank near Stratton Hall. Just upriver is the village of Levington and its creek, with inevitable barging associations. The narrow lanes round here do not invite casual parking, but if you can manage to stop somewhere near the friendly looking little brick church, or the Ship Inn immediately beside it, a brief excursion in search of the waterside and Levington's nature reserve may be worthwhile.

Immediately opposite the pub – built, so it is said, of old ship's timbers, and with smuggling connections that include Margaret Catchpole – is a public footpath. It emerges at the top of a field running down to the creek, guarded at this point by a lonely group of pines, a characteristic touch that reminds one that this is Suffolk, not Essex. But when I was last that way you could certainly see Essex from this vantage point, with the spire of Harwich church marking the skyline on the far side of the harbour.

Further upriver, one way of taking a first look at the port of Ipswich is from the 150 foot high Orwell Bridge, one of the seven wonders of the East Anglian world, which carries the A45 across the river a couple of miles below the docks. The parapet is too high to see over from a moving car, presumably to avoid accidents, but many people stop at one end or the other and walk up to enjoy the vertigo-inducing view.

The bridge had to be a high-level structure to enable Ipswich to continue expanding as a major port. Most of the recent development has been at the riverside quays, handling Baltic timber, grain, aggregates and general cargo. The Cliff Quay container terminal is on the east bank, and roll-on roll-off berths on the western side.

The enclosed wet dock at the head of the river, where fleets of meticulously maintained coasting spritsail barges used to lie at the millside wharves, is now a crowded yacht marina. For yachtsmen it is one of the special attractions of Ipswich that those ship-sized lock gates will open up for a puttering little pleasure boat, giving its helmsman that same feeling of undeserved respect one gets locking through the great Dutch sluices.

The Orwell bridge ... a 150 foot high wonder of the East.

The town's maritime history goes back a long way. The Romans were here, and the Danes. The Viking fleet which fought the Battle of Maldon had just finished sacking Ipswich. Canute landed here in 1016 to begin his conquest of England.

The medieval port did well out of the East Anglian wool trade and by the 17th century was making equally good use of Suffolk oak for extensive shipbuilding. In 1614 Ipswich was quoted as having more shipwrights than any other port in England. According to Defoe, they built a particularly fine breed of collier brigs. Reminiscing during his *Tour,* published in 1724, he recalled that 'just before the late Dutch Wars, Ipswich was a town of very good business; particularly it was the greatest town in England for large colliers or coal-ships, employed between New Castle and London: Also they built the biggest ships and the best, for the said fetching of coals of any that were employ'd in that trade: They built also there so prodigious strong, that it was an ordinary thing for an Ipswich collier, if no disaster happen'd to him, to reign (as seamen call it) forty or fifty years, and more.'

By the time Defoe was writing the port was in decline because its river was silting up. A 16 mile canal was dug to Stowmarket but never paid its way. By 1800 there was scarcely any water alongside the Ipswich wharves even at high tide. The local merchants realised that unless something was done, their port would soon be choked out of existence. Revival began in 1805 with the appointment of River Commissioners whose job it was to 'deepen, widen, cleanse and otherwise improve the river'. Trade recovered, harbour dues accumulated, and three decades later the Commissioners were able to propose the construction of a 33 acre dock on the north bank of the river. Its lock gates were opened for the first time in 1842, and for many years after that it was the largest wet dock in the country.

Apart from the absence of square-rigged masts and spritsails, the dock still looks more or less as it did in Victorian photographs. For a quick look round you can probably find somewhere to park on the south side looking across at the old Custom House which now provides offices for Associated British Ports. It was built in 1845 by the same architect who designed St John's church, Woodbridge – a fine, bold, self-consciously architectural building that makes much use of columns, vaults and balustrades. Though we describe it as 'old' it was really the new Custom House, built to serve and celebrate the magnificent new dock.

Among the few who did not apparently welcome the port's development was the Reverend Richard Cobbold, a member of the Ipswich brewing family, who in that same year published his novel *The History of Margaret Catchpole*. Recalling the river as Gainsborough and Constable knew it, he says regretfully:

'At the period we write of – the year 1792 – the Orwell's waves went boldly up to the port, as new and briny as in the days of the Danish invasion. Now they no longer wash the town. A wet-dock, with its embankments and its locks, shuts out the ebb and flow of the waters, and may be convenient to the inhabitants of the place; but sadly interferes with the early associations and recollections of those who, like the writer of this narrative, passed their boyish years upon the banks of the Orwell.'

Cobbold's novel is to Suffolk what the Reverend Baring-Gould's *Mehalah* is to Essex. Indeed the East Mersea clergyman may well have had his Suffolk counterpart's work in mind when he wrote his own. Both heroines are what we might now call 'liberated' women: strong-willed, independent, and with a suppressed sexuality which more domesticated Victorian readers could safely enjoy on the written page. The Reverend Cobbold made doubly sure of this respectability by larding his lurid tale with thick layers of moralising, but these can be ignored without too much difficulty.

Margaret Catchpole was a real Suffolk girl, befriended by the Cobbold family for whom she worked. By her own account she was persuaded by a man she met in Ipswich to ride a horse he had stolen from John Cobbold's stable to London, dressed as a man. In Shoreditch she was arrested trying to sell the horse. Although condemned to death at Bury Assizes in 1797, her sentence was commuted to seven years' transportation. Having been nevertheless left in Ipswich gaol, she made

The Custom House in Ipswich.

a spectacular and acrobatic escape three years later – in the novel it was to join her lover, the reformed smuggler Will Laud – only to be recaptured and sent off as a convict to Australia, where she was eventually released to run her own smallholding and died, unmarried, in 1819.

Richard Cobbold took these facts, plus his parents' stories about Margaret – such as how she saved young Master Henry from drowning – and embroidered them into an epic novel, Suffolk's own. In his story Margaret remains true to her smuggler, turning down an offer of marriage from honest John Barry, the Levington miller's son who becomes a Revenue officer. The climax is acted out on the North Sea beach at Shingle Street, where Barry's unfortunate sense of civic duty forces him to assist in Margaret's recapture just as she is about to escape with a repentant Laud to start a new life on the Continent. In the ensuing pistol duel, Laud is killed.

For all his unctuousness, the Reverend Cobbold gives full credit to Margaret's integrity and courage. He obviously enjoyed letting his imagination loose on the supporting characters, some of whom, like the half-crazy Orwell fisherman 'Robinson Crusoe', were drawn from life. And as Ronald Blythe points out in the Boydell Press edition, 19th century readers thoroughly familiar with horses must have found such a hard-riding heroine (she actually took 19 hours to ride the 'cropped strawberry roan gelding' the 70 miles to London, but Cobbold made it only 8½ hours) absolutely irresistible.

For myself, and I suspect others, much of the book's fascination comes from the use of detailed topography we can still recognise. Cobbold's characters are frequently to be found walking cross-country routes now known only to ramblers and conservation societies. Take this account of the lovers' escape:

'They fled to an empty cart-shed on the Woodbridge Road. Here Laud kept watch at the entrance whilst Margaret put on her sailor's dress. She soon made her appearance on the road with her white trousers, hat and blue jacket, looking completely like a British tar. They did not wait to be overtaken, but off they started for Woodbridge, and arrived at the ferry just as the dawning streaks of daylight began to tinge the east. Their intention was to cross the Sutton Walks and Hollesly Heath to Sudbourn. Unluckily for them, however, who should they meet at the ferry but old Robinson Crusoe, the fisherman, who, having been driven round the point at Felixstowe, was compelled to come up the Deben to Woodbridge, for the sale of his fish. The old man gave them no sign of recognition, but he knew them both, and, with a tact that few possessed, saw how the wind blew. But without speaking to either of them, he proceeded with his basket to the town.

'At this they both rejoiced, and as they took their journey across that barren tract of land, it seemed to them like traversing a flowery mead.'

Today we should have to take the A12; the Woodbridge ferry is closed; Sutton Common has an abandoned US airfield on it. But Margaret Catchpole's story is still a cracking good yarn.

Driving southwards out of Ipswich along the A137, the first clear view of the river is at Ostrich Creek, home of the Orwell Yacht Club.

Turning left at the Ostrich inn, the lower road along the shore, the B1456, offers the 'pretty' route to Manningtree via Holbrook and the obvious one to Woolverstone, Pin Mill and Shotley. About a mile or so after passing under the rising span of the Orwell Bridge, the road turns inland past Freston Park and its famous tower (which gave its name to another of Richard Cobbold's novels). This red-brick Tudor folly is actually a lot easier to spot from the river than from the road, but its story is worth telling anyway.

It was built in Henry VIII's time by Lord de Freston, who decreed that his daughter Ellen should spend a set period on each of its six floors, acquiring her various accomplishments. The day began at seven o'clock, with an hour devoted to 'charity' on the first floor, followed at nine by an hour's tapestry on the second floor, two hours of music on the third floor, and so on through painting and literature until two o'clock in the afternoon, when the wretched girl had a break until nightfall required her to resume with astronomy on the sixth floor.

Bear left at the next junction and you are soon in Woolverstone, where a sign directs you through the park to Woolverstone Marina and the friendly Royal Harwich Yacht Club. In winter particularly it is strange to find rows of boats hauled out, as it seems, in the middle of a wood. The trees open suddenly onto the Orwell at a place where the channel runs close to this shore: a good place for yacht moorings, but made uneasy by the wash of large ships passing to and from Ipswich docks.

On a low bluff near the RHYC clubhouse stands the Cat House, looking decidedly self-conscious in its stripped pink brickwork and 'gothic' windows. It was a landmark on the river long before there was a marina. When I first heard of it, and the cat in the window, it was supposed to have had smuggling associations, but Cobbold, writing Margaret Catchpole's story in the 1840s, gives a different explanation of its curious name:

'Woolverstone Park, with its thick copses and stately trees, whose roots reached, in snaky windings, to the very shore, was now the range along which the barque skirted till it came opposite to the white cottage, which stands on a small green opening, or lawn, slanting down to the river.

'The park boat was moored against the stairs, and a single light burned against the window, at which a white cat might be seen to be sitting. It was the favourite cat of the gamekeeper's, which had accidentally been killed in a rabbit-trap and, being stuffed, was placed in the window of the cottage. Visible as it always was in the same place, in the broad day and in the clear moonlight, the sailors on the river always called that dwelling by the name of the Cat House; by which it is known at the present day.'

To the right of the yacht club a signposted footpath runs through the riverside woods to Pin Mill – just far enough to sharpen thirst and appetite for a visit to the Butt and Oyster. At the bottom of a steep little lane from Chelmondiston, Pin Mill has always been a great favourite with East Coast yachtsmen, though again the passing ships make it an awkward anchorage. Its shingle hard is unusually long and wide, edged on the up-river side by a freshwater stream. You are almost sure to find a few sailing barges sitting there, attracting artists as well as sailors. This was once a great barging centre and latterly the home of Bob Roberts, who wrote several books about barges as well as skippering *Cambria*, the last to trade under sail.

Another bookish association, if you happened to read Arthur Ransome as a child, is with the adventures of *We Didn't Mean To Go To Sea,* which began from Alma Cottage by the hard. The last time I took a pint in the Butt and Oyster I was also pleased to see advertised E. Arnot Robertson's delightful novel *Ordinary Families,* set in Pin Mill at about the same period. Though this book was certainly written for adults, the families are seen through the eyes of a young woman growing up in a yacht-crazed family where she is the one who does not like sailing – a situation with which some readers may be familiar.

9

Yacht tenders await the tide at Waldring field.

THE DEBEN

FELIXSTOWE FERRY – WALDRINGFIELD – WOODBRIDGE – RAMSHOLT – BAWDSEY

MANY YACHTSMEN WOULD say that of all the rivers on the East Coast, the Deben is the most beautiful. From a sailor's point of view this river does seem to have almost everything: a fierce shingle bar to make you feel you have earned a quiet anchorage or a pint of beer; a fringe of salt marsh across which the waders drift and call; sandy bathing beaches; a renowned waterside pub at Waldringfield; and the handsome market town of Woodbridge with its spectacular Anglo-Saxon connections.

The river entrance is at Felixstowe Ferry a few miles north of Harwich. By road you approach down the A45 from Ipswich and then go left along the coast. It's called Felixstowe Ferry because there has long been a demand to cross at this narrow point, where one can embark and land on clean shingle. In the grand days of Bawdsey Manor, completed on the northern shore for the Quilter family in 1882, Sir Cuthbert Quilter even managed to organise a pair of steam-powered chain ferries across the entrance, one of which was named after Lady Quilter. In recent times a more modest service has been maintained by local watermen of the Brinkley family, who also acted as pilot and harbour master.

Felixstowe Ferry is an odd place, a great mound of shingle with deep water swirling and scouring past. The ebb tide, running at up to five knots, is even fiercer than the flood. It's a place to fish from or watch fishermen at work. Yachts pass so close to the beach, and so slowly when they are struggling against the tide, that you feel you can almost reach out and touch them. Yet they are in a completely different, and sometimes hostile, environment. Dinghies from the Felixstowe Ferry Sailing Club make light of the dangers, but deeper, heavier craft have often been in trouble on the bar, which shifts with every big gale.

Behind the beach just south of the entrance are two 'Martello towers', coastal forts built in Napoleonic times to repel a possible French invasion. You will see them at other places along this coast – Clacton, Shingle Street, Aldeburgh – and since they are marked on charts they provide yachtsmen with a useful measure of progress, whether sluicing past on the tide or plugging slowly against it.

Felixstowe Ferry at the mouth of the Deben.

Many people must have looked at Martello towers and wondered why and how they came to be in that particular place. One of Sir Walter Scott's characters suggested that they were erected 'for the sole purpose of puzzling posterity'. One answer is that many of the towers have been demolished. There were originally 102 along the shores of Sussex, Kent, Essex and Suffolk, many of them close enough to have overlapping fields of fire. So they must have covered most of the likely invasion spots. Certainly the military engineers who planned them had no doubt they would do the job.

They were built in imitation of a circular artillery fort on the Corsican Cape Mortella, which had managed to hold a Royal Navy squadron at bay in 1794. Although there were only 30 men inside the fort, with just three guns, they succeeded in driving off three British frigates with heavy casualties. Even when the British returned with 1,400 Marines and their own artillery, they only managed to dislodge the defenders after a lucky shot set fire to the tower.

The Admiralty was understandably impressed; this was obviously just the thing to repel Bonaparte. The British version was built of bricks, 700,000 for each tower, which must have been a tremendous boost for the local brickyards and cement works. The basic circular design was subtly improved to make it slightly egg shaped, with the narrow end towards the sea to deflect shells. The door was set high above ground for better defence. A 24-pounder long gun was positioned on the seaward parapet to engage the invasion fleet, with a pair of $5\frac{1}{2}$ inch howitzers, one on each side, to take care of the troops once they landed. It was reckoned that by using case shot, a tower could lay down the equivalent of a volley from two companies of infantry every few minutes.

The French in their turn were duly impressed; they called the English towers 'bull dogs'. As defences they were never put to the test and after Waterloo they rapidly became just historical curiosities, known irreverently in Suffolk as 'Mr Pitt's pork pies'.

About two-thirds of the way along the Deben's west bank is the tiny village of Waldringfield with its Maybush Inn, a small boatyard and a thriving sailing club. All three facilities are there for the same reason: at this point the river scours past a steep shingle beach where boats can land and launch cleanly at almost any state of the tide. The cartoonist Giles was among the thousands of yachtsmen who have come here each summer to race fleets of dinghies and keelboats, or moor their cruising boats to the buoys lining each side of the fairway.

Woodbridge, just off the A12 or at the top of 'Troublesome Reach' according to how you approach it, is a town full of history and with more than its share of fine buildings: medieval half-timbering, pink-red Georgian brickwork and yellow Victorian stocks. It's no longer a port as it was in Tudor times, when large vessels were built there. The town's remaining connection with the sea is through the yachting industry. In one respect it reminds me of Southwold, further north on the Suffolk coast: it conveys an atmosphere of discreet but long established prosperity that a stranger cannot easily explain, because there is no obvious source of wealth as there is in an industrial town or a major fishing port.

If you enjoy deciphering architectural patterns buy a historical guide (I found an excellent one by Carol and Michael Weaver) and you will find plenty of interest in these narrow streets. Sadly, the town was more or less cut off from its riverside in Victorian times by the construction of the railway. Instead it looks inward to the Market Hill square and the splendid Dutch-gabled Shire Hall, built in 1575 by Thomas Seckford, the town's famous benefactor. Edward FitzGerald, the eccentric Victorian man of letters and pioneering yachtsman who translated the *Rubaiyat of Omar Khayyam* from Persian, lived on the square above a gunsmith's shop for many years. He entertained Tennyson at The Bull nearby. Growing over his tomb at Bulge, on the far side of the Woodbridge bypass, is a primitive rose taken as a cutting from the rose on Omar Khayyam's grave.

The Tudor mansion (or Abbey) just off Market Hill was the family home of Thomas Seckford, a wealthy lawyer who managed somehow to serve both Mary Tudor and Queen Elizabeth. His original charity to Woodbridge was an almshouse, whose 19th century successors can

The Bell and Steelyard in Woodbridge.

be seen in Seckford Street at the other end of the square. They were built with wealth accumulated by Seckford's property in Clerkenwell, London – a connection I should perhaps have made for myself because I often visited a pub called the Seckforde Arms in Clerkenwell, near the *Guardian* newspaper's former offices.

From the opposite corner of the Woodbridge town square, New Street leads down past the Bell and Steelyard pub (the steelyard is an ancient balance crane jutting over the road, a spectacular device once used for weighing complete farm wagons on their way to and from the market). Follow the road past St John's Hill, scene of a 1915 Zeppelin raid, and you eventually emerge on the quayside. Opposite is the river bend on which the town's 18th century tide mill stands, beautifully restored in white weatherboarding. This is the tall shape that yachtsmen and painters both associate with Woodbridge. It dominates the waterfront, and the tide-filled pool that used to store water to turn its wheel has been converted into a marina.

A mill is believed to have stood on this site since the 12th century. This one was operating until 1956, the last of its kind in working order, when the wheel's great oak shaft broke. Dereliction set in until the 1960s, when funds were raised for restoration, and it is now open to the public during the summer. At certain times you can watch the machinery turning, driven by a newly built undershot wheel that takes its water from the small pool just upstream of the mill.

For hundreds of years a ferry used to run across the river from the adjacent quay. (It was here that Margaret Catchpole and her lover Will Laud supposedly crossed after her escape from Ipswich Gaol in 1800.) Indeed the ferry was of such ancient status that Parliament had to be consulted before it could be stopped. There is still a makeshift landing place on the far side of the river, from which footpaths lead up towards the Sutton Hoo burial site, but the National Trust does not welcome visitors by this route.

The royal possessions found in the Anglo-Saxon burial ship at Sutton Hoo have been described as the richest treasure ever dug from British soil. Excavation of the barrow began in 1939, disclosing the clearly moulded shape of an 80-foot clinker-built longship, apparently a working vessel because she had been noticeably repaired. There was just time to recover the horde of gold coins, ornaments, weapons and utensils that were to accompany the dead chieftain into the next world before war broke out in this one. The treasure was given to the British

The tide mill is the tall shape that yachtsmen and painters associate with Woodbridge.

Museum and has since been dated at around 625. Whether its owner was actually buried in his ship remained a mystery; he was almost certainly King Redwald. Public access to the site is from the B1083 Woodbridge–Bawdsey road.

Downstream from Woodbridge on the east bank of the Deben, the next easy access to the water is at Ramsholt. Not a particularly friendly place apart from its pub, but pretty. There is a grass-covered quay where yachtsmen leave their dinghies, a narrow strip of sand, and a small church on the hill with an oval tower built in Norman times, probably as a military strongpoint and lookout to which the church was then attached. From Ramsholt there is a pleasant walk upstream along the river wall to a little sandy cliff known to sailors as 'The Rocks' – a fine spot for bathing.

Driving down into Bawdsey, the road ends at the water, the deep, sluicing entrance to the River Deben. This is no ordinary Suffolk village. Until recently, the ferry quay was technically within the boundary of an important RAF station, built in the grounds of Bawdsey Manor. It was here in the 1930s that Robert Watson-Watt and his team developed the system of radio-location now known as radar.

Watson-Watt was in the great tradition of British boffins. Driving to Bawdsey from Orfordness, where the first radar experiments were conducted, his companion noted that the car had a fluid flywheel transmission that should theoretically enable the driver to go straight into reverse gear at 60 mph and simply wait for it to slow down and start going backwards. 'That's interesting', said Watson-Watt, 'shall we try it?' They did, and to their scientific delight – and perhaps surprise – it worked.

That trip in September 1935, recounted by the passenger in Gordon Kinsey's book *Bawdsey – Birth of the Beam,* led to the purchase of the manor from the Quilter family and the construction on the clifftop of a tall line of transmitting and receiving aerials, wooden structures that have since been dismantled. They were part of a chain of five stations, the others being Great Bromley and Canewdon in Essex, Dunkirk and Dover in Kent. The Germans knew something was up; they even sent the airship *Graf Zeppelin* snooping along the Suffolk coast, and were researching a system of their own. But Watson-Watt's team worked with a speed that seems astonishing in these bureaucratic days and by the time the Luftwaffe's bombers arrived there was a fully engineered radar chain looking out for them.

10

ORFORD HAVEN AND THE ALDE

SHINGLE STREET – ORFORD – ALDEBURGH – SNAPE

SHINGLE STREET IS what it says, a street of cottages sheltering from the east wind behind a great bank of shingle. Inland, most of the Suffolk countryside is so richly cultivated, so deeply secluded by its feudal past, it comes as something of a shock to emerge on this wild shore. No wonder Cobbold chose it for the climactic scene of his historical melodrama, when the smuggler Will Laud is shot down by the Revenue men as he is about to escape to sea with Margaret Catchpole. Even today this stretch of coast retains its feel of bleak isolation – the astringent lemon in affluent Suffolk's gin and tonic.

Approaching along the Hollesley road, park as soon as you reach the beach and trudge to the top of the shingle. You will be confronted by one of the most difficult and dramatic harbour entrances on the

East Coast. A haven certainly, but only when you have found the deep water of the river channel. On the bar the seas rarely subside, the shingle banks are always moving and the current runs at up to six knots on the ebb.

To your right as you face the sea, the first of the white cottages is the former Coastguard rescue station. Beyond the village is a row of early 19th century Martello towers, built with overlapping fields of fire as defence against a threatened Napoleonic invasion. To your left, farther along the beach, you should see the beacon which helps lead boats in across the bar from the buoy offshore.

From here the River Ore runs north for ten miles past Orford to Aldeburgh's Slaughden Quay, by which time Aldeburgh has claimed it as the River Alde, before winding inland for another six or seven miles to Snape Bridge. The river one would expect to flow into the sea at Slaughden, and which did for a few hours during the great 1953 flood, is actually diverted south by an extraordinary shingle spit that has slowly extended over many hundreds of years.

Until the 16th century the river entrance was miles away, more or less opposite Orford, once an important naval and commercial port which had grown up round its great Norman castle. The growth of Orfordness is a spectacular example of a phenomenon you will find all along the East Coast. The causes are complex: tidal streams clearly play some part, but the dominant factor is probably that the longest fetch for gales beating on this shore is from the north or northeast, and the size of waves is proportional to the fetch. Sand and shingle are lifted from one side of the ness and deposited on the other.

A short distance upstream the channel divides round Havergate Island, from the west side of which the Butley River runs inland for a few miles (it's really a creek, not a river and was known as such until recent times). There is a footpath down to the old barge quay there, a favourite anchorage for yachtsmen who like peace and quiet. At the upper end are oyster layings.

The channel inside Havergate Island is known as the Lower and Upper Gull. Believe it or not, a scheme was announced in 1813 to revive Orford as a major port serving the Baltic trade, which would have involved damming off the Gull, installing lock gates at the top end and cutting a new entrance from seaward through the spit. It all sounds highly unlikely now. Havergate has instead found fame as a bird reserve.

The island was probably formed between about 1530 and 1580 when Orfordness began to extend southwards across the entrance to the medieval harbour (a progression one can follow on the maps displayed in Orford Castle). Later it was drained to make good agricultural land, but some careless artillery during the Second World War let the sea back in and it was this that made it an ideal habitat for breeding avocets which were trying to re-establish themselves.

The avocet is perhaps the most elegant of all the wading sea birds, with a long curved beak tilted upwards at the tip instead of downward like the curlew's, to sweep for shrimps on the shore. It nested regularly along the East Coast until the early 19th century, when it was no doubt the fashion for stuffed birds and egg collecting that destroyed the population. In 1941 it returned to Norfolk and in 1947 to Suffolk, where two pairs bred at both Havergate and Minsmere. The island was purchased by the Royal Society for the Protection of Birds in the following year. Since then it has been developed as a sanctuary for the avocet and for many other species including various terns, the hen harrier and the short-eared owl. The RSPB adopted the beautiful avocet as its symbol, and the bird itself is now seen in many other places.

Havergate and the shingle spit of Orfordness, both approached by ferry from Orford Quay, have been jointly designated a national nature reserve. The shingle beach has many other associations, some of them far removed from the peaceable business of wildlife conservation.

One I have already mentioned: the dramatic climax of Margaret Catchpole's story, at least partly based on historical fact and recalling the violence of 18th century East Coast smuggling, when tens of thousands of gallons of illicit gin and brandy were run across the Suffolk beaches. During the First World War the spit became first a firing range and then an airfield, though why such an inconvenient place should have been chosen to operate a squadron of aircraft is not clear to me. Between the wars, as described earlier, Orfordness was used for the early experiments in the radio detection of aircraft – radar. Immediately after the Second World War the boffins returned, this time for secret work connected with the development of nuclear weapons. More recently, the US Air Force used the Lantern Marshes at the northern end of the spit for an experimental over-the-horizon radar, a great cat's cradle of wires which seemed to be more successful at interfering with ships' radios than in detecting ballistic missiles.

The name of the Lantern Marshes recalls the fact that Orfordness has been an important lighthouse site since the 17th century. A first pair of wooden huts, equipped with candle lights, seem to have been erected on the point in response to the disaster of 1627, when 32 ships were lost there in a single night. The huts were replaced by brick towers in 1720, after which a succession of lights were either burned down or washed away until 1792, when the present structure was built (accompanied until the late 19th century by a second, low light).

Orfordness may not be such a pivotal navigational point as it was then, when hundreds of collier brigs, hoys and smacks would sail past in a day. But the light's powerful flash, once every five seconds, is still a valuable navigational aid and Trinity House's proposal to decommission it within the next year or so has caused much disappointment. The lighthouse authority's argument is that since the lighthouse stands only yards from a fast eroding beach, it will in any case tumble into the sea within a few years, and moving it is not a practical option. The only small compensation is that the range of Southwold's light, further up the coast, will probably be increased by a few miles.

The village of Orford is quiet, fashionable, and dominated by two buildings begun in the same Norman period, the castle and the church. By road the approach is through either Rendlesham or Tunstall forest, badly devastated by the great storm of October 1987, and from which the B1084 leads straight into the little market square, with its celebrated Butley Oysterage and nearby smokehouse. You can see the castle to the right, or turn down past the church on to Quay Street, which did once have a small creek running alongside it. The present quay is at the far end past the riverside pub, now facing a car park instead of salt water, and beyond the hump which serves as a flood protection. A few fishing boats and the Orfordness ferry, as well as yachts, use the quay.

Orford Castle is still a magnificent structure, intelligently maintained as a public monument. Though only the keep remains, it fits any child's image of a castle, with turrets, cannons, a spiral staircase and a dungeon. For myself, I go back for the view from the battlements. After all, there are

Orford Castle, built by Henry II.

no real hills in East Anglia, but here is a chance to take in a vast expanse of marsh, shingle, sea and sky stretching from Shingle Street to Aldeburgh.

The castle was built for Henry II as a royal stronghold between 1165 and 1173, the first of its kind in this region. The garrison moved in even before the last stone was laid and within months the King's troops were under attack by an army of Flemish mercenaries raised by his rebellious son with one of the local barons. For a hundred years or so control of the fortress then passed back and forth between the monarchy and the barons. It was finally granted to Robert de Ufford in 1336 and remained in private ownership until 1930.

The keep is made of local septaria (Roman cement stone) faced with ashlar. The circular central structure is buttressed with three towers, in one of which is a spiral staircase. The other two contain small kitchens, bedrooms and a chapel leading off the central halls, the upper one of which is furnished with an enormous circular table that gives just a hint of medieval domesticity.

One of the nastier stories associated with the castle, dating from the time of Henry II, is that of the Orford 'merman'. God knows how the poor wretch came to be identified as that, but the legend is that he was caught by local fishermen in their nets, a naked hairy creature who did not speak even when taken to the castle, hung up by the heels and tortured. Time has transformed this gratuitous brutality into historical whimsy, and the story at least has a happy ending: the merman escaped back to the sea.

A church was begun at Orford at the same time as the castle, and although the present building is of a later date some of the Norman arches can still be seen at its eastern end. Musically, the church has associations with the composer Benjamin Britten and the nearby Aldeburgh Festival.

Past Orford Quay the River Ore runs fast and deep, an uneasy anchorage unless you have lots of heavy ground tackle. After two or three more bends it straightens out and becomes the River Alde for the last two miles to Slaughden Quay, Aldeburgh's riverside.

By road, Aldeburgh is most simply approached by turning off the A12 between Wickham Market and Saxmundham. It is really two towns in one. You drive in through 19th century Aldeburgh, much of it the work of the Garrett family, then drop down a steep slope past the church to join the top end of the High Street, running parallel with the beach. This narrow coastal strip beneath the cliff has developed from what remained of a more extensive medieval town. Centuries of coastal erosion have scoured away the shingle on which it was built until at its widest it can only provide room for three streets. Aldeburgh's most notable building, the Moot Hall, stood in the town centre when it was built in about 1500. Now it is only yards from the beach, relying on a concrete sea wall for its protection.

The Moot Hall has become the town's architectural symbol, though it is rather a muddle: a mixture of flint, brick, half-timbering and tile, with two tall Elizabethan-style chimneys at the south end which are not as old as they probably look. Not that it matters; the building has been used for many different purposes over the years (market, gaol, ammunition store, council chamber) which in retrospect seem to blend together. In summer it is open to the public.

Modern Aldeburgh is a comfortable watering place with smart musical connections and the best fish and chip shop for many a mile; an altogether softer environment than that described by its famous poet George Crabbe at the beginning of the 19th century. Yet the same east wind blows straight off the sea and some of the town's seafaring traditions are kept alive. Fresh fish is still landed and sold on the beach – even smoked there. The lifeboat is important on that stretch of coast and is still launched across the shingle as it always was, though nowadays any intervening banks built up by the last onshore gale are dug away by bulldozer rather than by teams of volunteers with shovels.

Along this coast lifeboats evolved naturally from the lug-rigged beach yawls that were already stationed there (the nautical equivalent of a modern motorway garage) both to serve and to exploit the vast fleets of clumsy square-riggers that worked their cargoes back and forth through the longshore channels. Collier brigs bringing fuel from Newcastle to stoke London's fires were counted not in tens but in hundreds. Hervey Benham quotes an account of one occasion in 1838 when nearly 2,000 vessels were windbound in Yarmouth Roads and then set sail southwards along the Suffolk coast all in the space of five hours.

The beach yawls that serviced this traffic were organised in 'companies', each with its own boat store and lookout tower. At Aldeburgh there were two rival companies, the 'Up-towners' and the 'Downtowners', with headquarters at the two towers you can still see standing on the beach. They would render any assistance that was required: putting a pilot aboard, supplying a replacement anchor, landing cargo. But of course they dreamed above all of lucrative salvage, in the process of which they often saved lives. The purpose of the lifeboats, as they became established in the 19th century, was to reverse these priorities, putting the life-saving first and the salvage second.

Aldeburgh's first lifeboat came from Sizewell gap just up the coast, now known for its nuclear power station. The boat was originally built for the Suffolk Shipwreck Association but moved south in 1851 and handed over to the Royal National Lifeboat Institution. Successive boats have become bigger, heavier and more powerful, but have never abandoned the traditional technique of launching off the beach.

It was in attempting to return through the surf that the Aldeburgh lifeboat suffered its worst disaster, in December 1899. She was broached and capsized by a heavy curling breaker, trapping six men who drowned before they could be extricated. A seventh member of the crew died later from his injuries. A monument to their courage stands by the east wall of Aldeburgh churchyard, alongside the simple stone crosses marking their graves. My sister Trixie, who taught at the Aldeburgh school, recalls taking a class to see the monument as part of their 'church project', only to find that instruction was superfluous: a number of the children were related to the names carved on the stones, and were well aware of it.

You will find three of the musical names associated with Aldeburgh and its festival in the newer section of the graveyard: Benjamin Britten, Peter Pears and Imogen Holst. The church itself is a sturdy Perpendicular building with wide aisles and no clerestory. Don't miss the window by John Piper at the far end of the North aisle in which three vivid panels

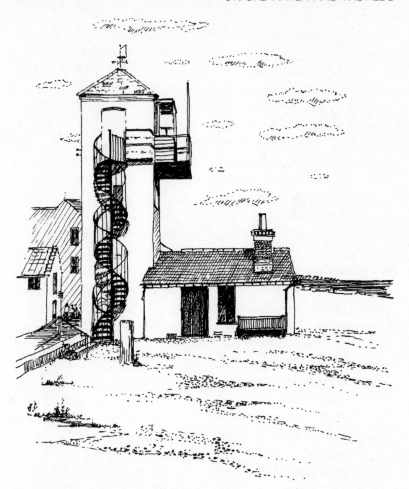

The lookout tower on the beach at Aldeburgh.

represent works by Britten: 'The Prodigal Son', 'Curlew River' and 'The Burning Fiery Furnace'.

If you are looking for fresh fish from the beach you will sometimes find it at this end of the town, more or less opposite the church. North from here along Crag Path, the houses soon give way to an open shingle bank separated from the marsh by the coastal road. If the season is right this is a good place to look for the special plants that enjoy this

135

salty shingle habitat: the blue flowered sea holly; pink rest harrow, so named because of the way its tough roots would catch the harrow; sea kale, which I am told was considered a delicacy, rather as samphire was on the Essex marshes; or sea pea, whose minute pods were gratefully accepted when there was little else to eat; and most dramatic of all, the yellow horned poppy.

Also at this end of the beach is a new, deeply controversial landmark: Maggi Hambling's 'Scallop' sculpture. Some admire its bleak visual impact; others disapprove, arguing that although words from one of Benjamin Britten's operas are cut into the metal shell ('I hear those voices that will not be drowned'), 'Ben' would not have been pleased; besides which there are no scallops round here.

Walking in the other direction from the Moot Hall, you will find Crag Path flanked by houses and hotels as far as the old Coastguard station, where it emerges on an open sea wall. Ahead is Aldeburgh's Martello tower, unique in its quatrefoil shape and the most northerly of the chain of similar fortresses. On your right is the River Alde, which on any other coast would make a sensible exit into the sea at this point instead of winding south for another ten miles to Shingle Street. Indeed the great tide of 1953 came close to establishing this more normal arrangement.

Slaughden Quay . . . Aldeburgh's riverside.

But for the moment, Orfordness remains attached to the mainland here by a narrow strip known as Slaughden.

Slaughden Quay has served as Aldeburgh's riverside at least since the alternative haven under Thorpeness disappeared, and in the past, though for a long while overshadowed by Orford further downriver, it was a major port. The poet George Crabbe knew it only in decline. By 1810, when he described his home town in 'The Borough', the whole length of its seaward shoreline had been under creeping attack for two centuries or more. Whole streets of houses had been washed away including, in 1779, the house in which he was born, the son of a saltmaster at Slaughden. Economic depression accompanied the encroaching sea, but the river still provided a sheltered anchorage for 'hoys, pinks and sloops; brigs, brigantines and snows'.

Crabbe was criticised in his day for being insufficiently 'poetical'. He refused to sentimentalise about the rigours of rural life, and was interested enough to write a long descriptive poem covering every aspect of his own community. He must have been one of the first writers to acknowledge that mudflats and saltings have their own esoteric beauty:

> Here samphire-banks and salt-wort bound the flood,
> There stakes and sea-weeds withering on the mud.

It was Crabbe's portrayal of the cruel embittered fisherman Peter Grimes, one of 'The Poor of the Borough', which inspired Britten to write his opera 'Peter Grimes':

> When tides were neap, and, in the sultry day,
> Through the tall bounding mud-banks made their way,
> Which on each side rose swelling, and below
> The dark warm flood ran silently and slow;
> There anchoring, Peter chose from man to hide,
> There hang his head and view the lazy tide
> In its hot slimy channel slowly glide;
> Where the small eels that left the deeper way

For the warm shore, within the shallows play;
Where gaping mussels, left upon the mud
Slope their slow passage to the fallen flood;
Here dull and hopeless he'd lie down and trace
How sidelong crabs had scrawled their crooked race;
Or sadly listen to the tuneless cry
Of fishing gull or clanging golden-eye;
What time the sea-birds to the marsh would come,
And the loud bittern, from the bull-rush home,
Gave from the salt-ditch side the bellowing boom.

As far as I know Britten did not include the bittern's 'boom' in his score, but he did use the characteristic groan and grunt of a distant foghorn to add a touch of nautical realism to the last climactic scene. It is something that had always puzzled the musician Dr W. H. Swinburne, a family friend who like Britten had spent his boyhood in Lowestoft. Why include a foghorn when there is no such thing at Aldeburgh? Could the composer have been recalling the old Low Light at Lowestoft, which did have a fog signal?

My own guess, after consulting Trinity House, is that the adult Benjamin Britten was familiar with the sound of the Shipwash light vessel, then stationed about six or seven miles from Aldeburgh off Orfordness. At the beginning of Act III, Scene 2 the score of 'Peter Grimes' shows a long E flat dropping to D natural, which I take to represent the grunting type of foghorn known as a diaphone. The real Grimes could never have heard a diaphone because it was not used until the mid-1920s, when the first in this district was installed on the Outer Gabbard light vessel, also off Orfordness, but a lot further out. Later the Shipwash was also converted. But as far as I can tell the Lowestoft Low Light, which remained in use until 1923, always had either a bell or a horn.

Slaughden still has its quay, with a couple of boatyards. Alongside are the Aldeburgh Yacht Club and Slaughden Sailing Club, with racing fleets of Dragons and 'vintage' Loch Longs. From there the river winds inland, past an old brickworks jetty at the back of the town and out into Long Reach, where the mudflats stretch for half a mile on either side. The north shore at this point is known locally as 'Little Japan', presumably because the flat-topped pines are reminiscent of a Japanese print.

Black Heath Wood, with Hazelwood Common and Snape Warren on either side, forms the route of the most notable walk in this area, the 'Sailor's Path'. As its name suggests, it is the cross-country route sailors would take back to Aldeburgh if their ships were delayed loading or neaped at Snape Bridge. The river views recall the equivalent walk from Blythburgh to Walberswick.

To join the Sailor's Path from Aldeburgh, take the A1094 out of the town and past the Golf Club, then pull in on the left just before an isolated postbox. The route is marked by posts. At the far end you will find yourself at the corner of a narrow lane, from which in dry conditions you can cut down to the river, I am told, and reach Snape Bridge along the sea wall. The more obvious alternative is to walk straight ahead and through the village.

Snape Bridge, carrying the B1069 road, marks the end of the navigable River Alde, although the non-tidal waterway extends inland for many more miles. High tide here is two and a half hours later than at Shingle Street.

By water, the approach from Aldeburgh twists through Troublesome Reach (closely equivalent to the River Deben's reach of this name), past Iken Cliff and through reed beds to the tall quay alongside the Snape Maltings; an awkward channel to negotiate if you are unfamiliar with it, but the sailing barges used to manage perfectly well, as witnessed by the inn sign of the Plough and Sail, and small motor barges brought in grain from Tilbury for some time after that.

The Maltings no longer produce malt. Instead, the steep tiled roofs and square white ventilators are famous as the unlikely concert hall of the Aldeburgh Music Festival, founded by Benjamin Britten and the singer Peter Pears in 1948. By the mid-1960s the festival had outgrown the parish churches in which it began and one of the Snape buildings was converted, quite simply and very successfully, into a concert hall. The Queen opened it for the twentieth Festival in 1967. Two years later it was burned out, but reopened in even better shape for the 1970 Festival. More recently it was the setting for the two-year inquiry into the Sizewell B nuclear power station project, the longest public inquiry ever held.

Perhaps the ideal way to visit Snape if you happen to be interested in both music and boats is to sail there for a concert, though you will be extremely lucky to get away on the same tide. But there are plenty of other things going on: shops, galleries, musical workshops, a café, boats coming and going at high tide. The riverside path back to Iken and its church is well trodden. Or you can just take a pint at the Plough and Sail and wander round the mellowed collection of buildings Newson Garrett created there in the 1840s and 1850s.

The name of Garrett crops up throughout this area; for instance the Leiston ironworks belonged to the family. Newson Garrett arrived at Snape in 1841 to begin shipping out corn, and established the maltings a few years later. They say he scratched the line of the frontage in the dust with his stick and told his workmen to build it there. He was the archetypal Victorian industrialist – aggressively enterprising, imaginative, irascible – and welcomed the Great Eastern Railway, for which he built the tall brick arch at the front. His eldest daughter Elizabeth Garrett Anderson also had a lot of spirit, becoming the first woman Doctor of Medicine and Mayor of Aldeburgh, while her younger sister Millicent was the suffragette who married the blind MP Professor Fawcett.

Dunwich beach.

SOUTHWOLD AND THE BLYTH

DUNWICH – WALBERSWICK – BLYTHBURGH – SOUTHWOLD

> Swoul and Dunwich, and Walberswick,
> All go in at one lousie creek.

ONE GLANCE AT THE tide boiling round the narrow entrance to Southwold Harbour is enough to convey the depth of feeling behind this old North Seamen's rhyme, quoted by Defoe in the early 1700s. After centuries of rivalry, Southwold had by then appropriated the harbour from its neighbours as winter gales shifted the entrance northwards. And for centuries since it has been 'lousie' in the sense of being awkward to negotiate and not exactly spacious inside. I recall once rushing out with my small son Jim to witness the rare event of a tiny coaster, a proper ship, entering the harbour – she rammed the pier we were standing on and bounced in off the other. In yachts at different times I have had to be towed in by a powerful fishing boat to overcome the fierce ebb, and knocked off a large chunk of stern on the north pier trying to beat out against a rising easterly gale.

If on the other hand the word 'lousie' merely means that the creek is infested with green shore crabs, then I can vouch for that too. My kids used to catch hundreds of them by dangling bacon rind over the wooden footbridge behind Walberswick beach.

That muddy little gutway running parallel with the beach is a vestigial reminder that the River Blyth used to flow into the sea a lot farther south, firmly within the jurisdiction of Dunwich rather than Southwold. When you visit the prosperous Victorian-built resort of Southwold today, with just a few plump little fishing boats tethered at the river staging, you are looking at the inheritor of more than a thousand years of maritime history which began in a city now almost totally disappeared beneath the North Sea.

The recorded history of Dunwich dates from the 7th century, when the East Anglian King Sigbert established himself there and brought Christianity with him. The city reached a peak of prosperity in the 12th century, during the reign of Henry II (for whom Orford castle was built), and a century later it was still the biggest port in Suffolk with 80 ships of its own. But coastal erosion was already eating away the sandy cliffs and silting the river entrance. A long struggle began to maintain the harbour, and hence the right to levy dues on shipping from the other three communities that shared it: neighbouring Walberswick, Blythburgh at the head of the estuary, and Southwold on what was then an island opposite.

The wealth which paid for Blythburgh's magnificent 15th century church was founded as much as anything on Suffolk wool; the three coastal towns combined commerce with inshore fishing and shipbuilding. From the 13th century onwards they also contributed to an East Coast fleet of Iceland 'barks' and fishing vessels which sailed for the Arctic each spring to trade goods and return with supplies of salted cod and ling. To begin with, Dunwich was the dominant partner in this remarkable venture. But as its shoreline crumbled and the river entrance drifted away, first Walberswick – at its peak in the 15th century – and then Southwold, gained the upper hand. By the 16th century Southwold was sending more ships to Iceland than any of the East Coast ports.

As far as the harbour was concerned, Dunwich's effective downfall came on 14 January, 1328, when a great storm blocked the river entrance and the pent-up water broke through to the sea two miles farther north, not so far from where you see it today. Yet Dunwich did not give up quickly or easily. The arguments went on for many more years; ships were sunk, sailors murdered. But by 1488 Southwold did finally stop paying harbour dues to its rival and in 1590 it combined with Walberswick to cut the present entrance.

Medieval Dunwich was doomed anyway. Since Roman times about a mile of land has been eaten away and for the past four centuries erosion has averaged about a metre a year. So the tiny village you see today is no more than the remnant of a great lost city.

In *Dunwich Suffolk* Jean and Stuart Bacon record no less than twelve vanished churches. Some were swept away as the marshes flooded, others toppled over the cliffs. The diving expeditions in which the Bacons were involved uncovered a few traces of them, and Dunwich Museum tells their story. But for the most part all that remains are sailors' tales of ghostly submerged bells ringing at the turn of the tide.

The last of the old churches, All Saints, was poised on the clifftop within living memory. In 1904 it began to collapse, accompanied by a macabre process of disinterment. The last section of the West tower crashed over in 1919, though one of the buttresses was removed and re-erected in St James's churchyard.

Today, the most prominent local seamark is the white dome of Sizewell B nuclear power station (Britain's first American-style PWR). It may soon be joined by another, renewing argument between those who see it as a sensible response to climate change and opponents who fear it could be East Anglia's answer to Fukushima. Meanwhile, a small but active fishing fleet works from the nearby beach.

Shrouded behind a dark forestry plantation off the Westleton–Blythburgh road is the small modern village of Dunwich, welcoming tourists at the Ship Inn, a museum (only open in the summer) and a beach café. Climb the beach from the car park and you may still see one or two fishing boats canted against the North Sea horizon.

Immediately south of the village, Dunwich Heath and Westleton Walks provide a network of footpaths through gorse, birch and pine: fine walking country leading across to Eastbridge and the Eels Foot Inn. This marshy pub, where dragoons once laid in wait for the smugglers, is now on the landward edge of the 1,500 acre Minsmere nature reserve, run by the Royal Society for the Protection of Birds and one of the most successful in the country. Here they preserve a breeding habitat for threatened rarities like the marsh harrier, bittern, bearded tit and little tern.

Approaching Walberswick along the Blythburgh road, you can either cut across the forest to come out at the old centre of the village, or carry on to turn right at the water tower. This road follows the River Blyth through an area of heath known as Tinker's Walks (famous as the haunt of adders) until you reach the wrought-iron ship sign that marks the start of Walberswick.

This route is well worth retracing on foot, branching off halfway back to Blythburgh to take the path through the riverside woods that comes out in the village. On the other side of the A12 is Blythburgh church, surely one of the finest in East Anglia. In style it is boldly Perpendicular, with 36 clerestory windows lighting the long nave. Work started in 1412 and took 80 years, incorporating an earlier steeple. This proved a dangerous expedient, because in 1577 a great storm 'cleft the door, and returning to the steeple, rent the timber, brake the chimes, and

Blythburgh ... with one of the finest churches in East Anglia.

fled towards Bongay, six miles off'. To make matters much worse, all this happened during a service. The steeple crashed through the roof, killing two of the congregation and leaving lightning scorch marks on the north door which are still visible, made, so it was said, by the Devil's fingers as he clawed his way out.

Dowsing and his henchmen came this way in 1644, to smash the statues and loose off their muskets at the wooden angels in the roof. They stabled their horses between the pillars of the nave, where two of the iron rings to which they were tethered can still be seen. Either because of the Reformation, or because Blythburgh in its economic decline did not need such a large church, the building seems to have been generally neglected from then until the second half of the 19th century, by which time windows had been roughly bricked up and the congregation sat under umbrellas to keep off the rain dripping through the roof. With the structure on the brink of collapse, a restoration fund was started in 1881 and the work has gone on ever since. On 12 August, 1944 the old church was shaken by another bolt from the heavens, which loosened the leaded clerestory windows. A US bomber passing overhead had exploded, detonating its 12-ton load of high-explosive bombs. On board was Joseph Kennedy, eldest brother of the presidential Kennedy family.

Suffolk has retained its wartime links with the US Air Force, and it was American generosity which enabled six missing angels' wings to be replaced in 1954. The bright colours which once decorated the rest of the roof have faded to soft green, red and yellow on a chalky white background. Combining with the pink red of the brick floor, the effect is of warmth and light. For me, a return visit to this 'cathedral of the marshes' is never a disappointment.

Walberswick's church, on the left as you enter the village, was built at the same time as Blythburgh's Holy Trinity and to very much the same design – but no-one stepped in to save it. On the contrary, valuable items like lead roofing and bells were sold off as the town's fortunes rapidly declined. The present structure, a modest shelter inside a much grander ruin, is a reminder of how far what was once an important

Walberswick ... once an important seafaring town.

seafaring town has come down in the world. But in another sense the opposite is true. Having returned to its humble origins as a fishing village, Walberswick has more recently acquired a smart new reputation as a discreet holiday resort, full of good taste and money. In this guise it is sometimes disparagingly referred to as 'Hampstead-on-Sea'. For families particularly, it nevertheless offers a charming combination of sea, sand dunes, marsh and river.

Beyond the green, with its art galleries, you come out on the riverside behind the harbour entrance. Tucked in on the right is the Bell Inn, in my experience always a lively, friendly sort of pub. Nearby Valley Farm was for some years the home of the English impressionist painter Philip Wilson Steer (1860–1942), whose view of Walberswick seems to have been pleasantly filled by pretty girls strolling along the beach.

The large car park beyond the Bell is still sometimes referred to as the 'fishermen's flats' because this was where the fishing nets were laid out on trestles to dry, rather as they were on the Denes at Lowestoft. The larger quayside sheds are now used as holiday cottages, but smaller ones up-river are decorated with orange netting and rusty beam trawls which suggest they are still serving their original purpose.

The harbour entrance itself symbolises a partnership in which Walberswick is clearly the junior. Whereas the solid north pier has the effect of retaining a broad sandy beach along the Southwold shore, the open concrete lattice on the southern side seems to do nothing to prevent the steady scouring of Walberswick's beach. In fact the lattice pier is important in reducing the switchback effect which used to make the harbour even more uncomfortable, and for small boat sailors it is reassuring to note that the current always flows inward through the piles, whatever the tide is doing. Inside the harbour, the northern quayside has recently been rebuilt to provide a base for the RNLI's inshore lifeboat and, it is hoped, commercial vessels of one kind or another.

To reach the Southwold side you may be lucky enough to find the riverside ferry working, part-time successor to the grandly named River Blyth Ferry Company which in its latter days operated a tall-funnelled steamboat. The alternative is to walk round across the bridge about a mile upstream.

This crossing also has a more distinguished history. The swing bridge which stood there until it was demolished during the Second World War (presumably as a precaution against invasion), was the pride of the old Southwold Railway. The railway was built in 1878, when every smart seaside town had to have one. It branched off the Great Eastern Railway at Halesworth, crossed the river to serve Wenhaston, then passed under the A12 at Blythburgh and along the riverside to Walberswick Common. According to local historians, rolling stock consisted of redundant Chinese tramcars (with free straw to keep your feet warm on cold days) and a trio of little tank engines that sometimes had to be helped up the Halesworth incline by a team of horses (Jean and Stuart Bacon tell the full story in their booklet on Southwold).

Once across the modern bridge you are on Southwold's Blackshore, where the Harbour Inn proudly displays the 1953 flood level halfway up its wall. Along this bank, moored to every kind of improvised staging, you will find yachts belonging to the Southwold Sailing Club alongside the remaining three or four vessels of the town's fishing fleet.

'Hereabouts', as Defoe remarked in his 18th century *Tour,* 'they begin to talk of herrings, and the fishery . . . here also they cure sprats in the same manner as they do herrings at Yarmouth; that is to say, speaking in their own language, they make red sprats; or to speak good English, they make sprats red.'

Defoe was writing just before Southwold made its first effort to turn the traditional inshore fishing into a large-scale commercial industry, which was in turn part of a national campaign to challenge Dutch control of the North Sea herring fishery. With the harbour's first pier just completed, the Free British Fishery was established at Southwold in 1750. A fleet of herring 'busses', 70 foot square-rigged sailing drifters, was ordered, and for a few years the town's inns and workshops enjoyed an economic boom as the ships were sent off each summer to join the Dutch off the Shetlands and follow the shoals south.

By the time Southwold tried again, in the early years of the century, Yarmouth and Lowestoft were already prospering at the centre of a vast North Sea fishery, their quays crowded with drifters and trawlers. The awkward little harbour on the River Blyth was designated by the Board of Trade as a kind of nautical overspill. A contemporary photograph shows a pair of girls Wilson Steer might have admired, arm in arm, swinging their skirts along the refurbished quay to welcome the first vessel to range alongside.

Southwold boasted that it was going to 'drive Lowestoft into the sea', and for a time it did become another port of call for the migratory Scottish luggers. Herring and sprats were cured as of old, and exported to Germany. But the harbour was never really sorted out, and it never

Two's company . . . Southwold harbour.

had a proper railway. In the end Southwold had to rest content with the new prosperity it had discovered as a fashionable seaside resort in the late Victorian years, elegant summer residences overlooking the green, bathing machines on the beach.

That is basically the town we see today, and very handsome too. Approaching Southwold by road, turn off the A12 just north of the River Blyth crossing. The bridge you cross just as you enter the town, Might's Bridge, is a reminder that in medieval times Southwold was an island, separated from the mainland by Buss Creek, now little more than a ditch. It was evidently named after the herring busses mentioned earlier, an early form of fish factory ship, which used to shelter there when it was open to the sea.

The road leads straight to the Market Place, marked by the triangular town pump decorated with fish, crown and arrows. It's a fine piece of work in cast iron, reminiscent of the dolphin lamps lining the Victoria Embankment in London, though as the authors of the architectural guide *Discovering Southwold* remark, these dolphins are quite definitely herrings. 'Defend They Ryghts', the pump's motto advises.

From the Market Place the road forks. To the left are the crowded streets surrounding East Green by the lighthouse, and Bartholomew's Green on which stands the 15th century parish church of St Edmund. To the right a much larger green area opens up. It was cleared by the disastrous fire of 1659 which destroyed almost the whole town, but eventually provided this spacious, grassy setting for fine Regency and Victorian villas that convey Southwold's latter-day prosperity.

On the seaward side is Gun Hill with its six iron cannon, given to the borough by the Board of Ordnance in 1746, probably as a defence against French privateers. In the First World War they were buried out of sight after German warships bombarded the apparently fortified town. In the next war they were once again hidden, this time to avoid joining miles of the East Coast's iron railings as scrap metal.

Beyond the greens Ferry Road leads down to the harbour mouth and the riverside. Looking back at the town, the skyline is shaped by the white lighthouse tower and the grey flintwork of St Edmunds, both about a hundred feet high. The lighthouse is even more striking at close quarters, overpowering the neat Victorian brickwork of Corn Field Terrace or rising suddenly into view above the roof of the Sole Bay Inn. It was built in the 1880s by the same Trinity House engineer who designed Cromer and Hunstanton lights, and was converted to electricity in 1938. Its white light is visible for 18 miles from seaward (soon perhaps increasing to 24 miles), with red sectors warning vessels clear of coastal sandbanks off Lowestoft and Sizewell.

The church of St Edmund is from the 15th century like those at Walberswick and Blythburgh, and decorated with some especially fine flintwork. Like Blythburgh's Holy Trinity it has a 'Jack-o-the-clock', known here as Southwold Jack and adopted as the symbol of the nearby Adnams Brewery. Jack is a small wooden soldier, who when a rope is pulled strikes a bell mounted on the wall. His ecclesiastical function is to announce the beginning of services, the arrival of a bride at her wedding and so on. Historically, his interest is that he precisely depicts the equipment and clothing of a contemporary soldier – that is one who fought in the Wars of the Roses.

Beneath the Jack is a chunk of timber from the old belfry carved with the name of 'Harrye Cocke 1584', the suggestion being that he did it to while away the time as he watched for the Spanish armada. If so, he had a long wait. But church towers such as this must have been much more important as vantage points than they are today, and it may well be that when the Dutch fleet hove into view in 1672 to engage the English in the great battle of Sole Bay, the first sighting was from here. It must have been a fearful moment because many of the English warships anchored in the bay had their crews ashore, the Dutch Admiral de Ruyter was bearing down with a fleet of 130 ships (the English and the French between them had 150), and whatever happened this was going to be a bloody encounter. As indeed it was, though indecisive. Bodies were washed ashore for a long time afterwards.

The battle is naturally an important theme for the Southwold museum, housed in a little Dutch gabled cottage opposite the church.

The lighthouse behind the Sole Bay Inn is visible 18 miles from seaward.

There are paintings of it, charts, and copies of van der Velde's sketches. Other exhibits include a ship's medicine chest, old railway equipment and the whipping post that used to stand on the green outside. One charming feature when I last looked inside was a summer display of freshly gathered wild flowers, labelled like any other exhibit.

At the seaward end of East Street is a remarkable Southwold institution, the Sailors' Reading Room, which though it acts as a kind of maritime museum, still serves something like its original purpose. I choose my words cautiously because according to the authors of *Discovering Southwold*, the intention of the naval widow who paid for it in 1864 was 'to wean the fishermen from their alleged failings – going to sea on the Sabbath and getting drunk on any day of the week.' Casual visitors may look round the outer room which is stuffed with nautical photographs, paintings and models. Gazing seawards above the card table are buxom, heavy chinned ships' figureheads painted shiny blue, mauve and pink. There is also a superbly crafted model of the last and probably the fastest of the Southwold beach yawls, the 49-foot *Bittern*, built in 1890. Her narrow rudder is mounted outside.

The beach yawls of Suffolk and Norfolk must have been quite amazing craft: finely drawn, undecked, clinker-built double-enders up to 70 feet long, rigged with twin lugsails, and looking like distant descendants of the Viking longships. The smaller ones at least would launch straight off the shingle. Dipping the forward lugsail in heavy weather must have required perfect teamwork, especially since the bags of shingle ballast that kept them upright had to be shifted across the bilges at just the same moment before her sails filled on the new tack. A contemporary account suggests they could be sailed with the lee gunwhale six inches below water level with only a trickle coming aboard, such was their speed. This speed was an essential part of their function – remember they were working boats, not yachts – because although they did a lot of routine fetching and carrying, they were built by rival beach companies ultimately to compete for the lucrative salvage prizes. In the process, they also saved many lives.

One prize that eluded the 69-foot Yarmouth beach yawl *Reindeer*, along with many other hopeful challengers, was the America's Cup. She offered to take on the original schooner *America*, but the US visitors wanted more money than the Yarmouth company could afford to stake. Who knows what might have happened in a good reaching breeze from off the land, with the Scroby Sands waiting to trip the schooner's keel?

12

LOWESTOFT

IT WAS DANIEL DEFOE who wondered why the bold River Waveney should turn timidly north to join the Yare after so nearly breaking through to the sea at Lowestoft. 'No one would doubt', he wrote in 1724, 'but that when they see the river growing broader and deeper, and going directly towards the sea, even to the edge of the beach; that is to say, within a mile of the main ocean; no stranger, I say, but would expect to see its entrance into the sea at that place, and a noble harbour for ships at the mouth of it.'

The fact is that the natural mouth of the Waveney valley forming Oulton Broad and Lake Lothing (the inner harbour) had for centuries been intermittently blocked by a shingle bank, just as smaller valleys along the Suffolk coast still are today. But Defoe knew how jealously Yarmouth guarded its commercial monopoly as the sole access to the inland port of Norwich, and he seems to have sensed that the Suffolk men might one day strike back.

It took almost exactly a hundred years. And then the initiative came not from Lowestoft but from the Norwich merchants, annoyed by the way they felt Yarmouth took advantage of its navigational stranglehold.

The New Cut was dug from Reedham to Haddiscoe to avoid Yarmouth's Breydon Water, a double facing lock was installed at Mutford Bridge below Oulton Broad and a channel cut through the shingle beach. The pent-up waters of Lake Lothing were released to scour the harbour entrance for the first time in 1831. A few months later the first collier brig entered the new harbour and two years later the same vessel delivered coal all the way to Norwich by the Lowestoft route (a full account of this great engineering venture can be found in Wilfrid Wren's *Ports of the Eastern Counties*).

Though this initial effort to bypass Yarmouth gave Lowestoft its existence as a harbour, it was the coming of the railway in the 1840s, brought there by the enterprise of Samuel Morton Peto, which turned it into a busy fishing port and holiday resort. Peto, who appropriately was also responsible for Nelson's Column in Trafalgar Square, was in the heroic tradition of Victorian civil engineering. In three years he had organised a railway link from Reedham complete with sidings to the fish quay, built an extensive harbour to shield and develop the new entrance, and laid the foundations of an elegant new promenade immediately south of the harbour.

Approaching Lowestoft from London along the A12 (though the railway from Ipswich, known locally as 'the rattler', is an attractive alternative) you enter the town behind the Victorian seafront to emerge at the harbour's lifting bridge, with the Royal Norfolk and Suffolk Yacht Club immediately on your right. As good a way as any to take a first view of the place, if you can find somewhere to park this side of the bridge, is to walk out along the south harbour pier to the little pagoda-shaped tower at the pierhead. The basic layout of the town as seen from there is still much as Peto created it.

Looking back to your left you have the handsome villas of what was once boastfully described as 'probably the finest promenade in the United Kingdom', offering its wealthy residents 'a noble view of the German Ocean'.

Immediately in front of you is the yacht harbour, which also provides a convenient mooring for the lifeboat, and the Edwardian clubhouse of the Royal Norfolk and Suffolk Yacht Club. It was designed in 1902 – just the right setting for the long-skirted but emancipated young

The Royal Norfolk and Suffolk Yacht Club.

women who were already part of the local yachting scene at that time. Yet although visiting yachtswomen are now of course warmly welcomed, the club remained for many years an unyielding bastion of male chauvinism. Female members were allowed to race yachts, but not use the clubhouse. Then in the early 1920s so many of the club's 'Brown Boats' were owned by ladies, they insisted on attending the annual owners' meeting – a privilege reluctantly conceded provided they entered the room by way of the balcony, up an iron staircase.

The varnished Brown Boats are possibly the oldest one-design class in the country. Known more properly as Broads One-Designs, they are 24 feet long, spoon-bowed with a gunter sloop rig. The design was commissioned from Linton Hope in 1900, his brief being to produce a boat that would be equally at home on the inland Broads and on the open sea off Lowestoft. He did just that, and the class has been enthusiastically raced ever since (outlasting the more beautiful Dragons, that are no longer raced here). Nearly all the Brown Boats are named after birds, just as the Norfolk 'White Boats' take the names of butterflies.

The powerful blue-hulled RNLI lifeboat usually lying in the corner of the yacht harbour is the latest in an extremely long line. Lowestoft

Lake Lothing.

is one of the oldest lifeboat stations in the British Isles, a measure of the respect with which the offshore sandbanks, the Corton and the Newcombe, have always been regarded.

The first lifeboat was placed here in 1801, 23 years before the Royal National Lifeboat Institution itself was founded. It was built by Henry Greathead of South Shields, who only twelve years earlier had built the first lifeboat of all, the *Original*. His Lowestoft design was a 30 foot double-ender driven by twelve oars, and the local beachmen did not like her. So in 1807 the Suffolk Humane Society had another boat built for them in the town, the *Frances Anne*, and this time fitted her with sails. In this respect Lowestoft really did set the precedent. The *Frances Anne* became the forerunner of a long succession of sailing lifeboats to serve the RNLI, the last of them not retired until 1948 when fishing under sail was also dying out. She saved 300 lives, and set the style for a class of lifeboat that guarded the Norfolk and Suffolk coasts for many subsequent generations.

Inside the lifting town bridge that carries the A12 is the mile-long Lake Lothing, which leads through, via two more movable bridges and a lock, to Oulton Broad. This inner harbour (Lake Lothing, not the broad) is the home of the Lowestoft Cruising Club and the scene of much commercial shipping activity – but few places from which to inspect it. Altogether a gloomy stretch of water, a retirement home for old ships and trawlers that are past their survey date, and for some of them a permanent graveyard.

The north side of the outer harbour contains the trawl dock – rarely used these days – and beyond that Hamilton Dock, effectively a marina with berths for a few inshore fishing vessels, yachts, and a couple of

Lowestoft fish harbour.

wind farm support vessels. The big deep-sea trawlers that were once such a feature of this port have gone.

Northwards beyond the harbour, Lowestoft's High Street climbs along the cliffs towards the lighthouse, with a modern industrial estate on the flat shore below. The grassy sand dunes between cliff and beach, or what is left of them, are known here as the Denes (presumably another way of spelling 'dunes'). They are linked to the High Street above by a series of 'scores': steep paved alleyways running down the cliffs, some with steps at the top, with names like Herring Fishery Score, Mariner's Score and Lighthouse Score.

The southern end of the Denes next to the harbour, where factories now sprawl and a lofty wind turbine represents the town's latest industrial activity, was the site of the 19th century Beach Village. As the fisheries expanded so did the village, a collection of brick and flint cottages that eventually acquired their own church – and thirteen pubs! It was a distinct community within the town, consisting of longshoremen, those fishermen who didn't do well enough to buy houses on top of the cliff, and the families who supported the fishing fleets by working in the markets, smokehouses and net stores. Posts on which teams of local girls would stretch the drift nets for treating, drying and mending still stand further along the shore. An elderly friend who lived at the top of Lighthouse Score as a child remembers the vitality of the place: the tiny houses decorated with seashells, names like Anguish Street (in memory of some fishermen drowned in the harbour mouth), and the running fights up and down the scores as the pubs emptied.

The Beach Village became derelict during the Second World War and much of it was swept away by the 1953 floods, doing the post-war town planners' work for them. But it's worth driving down Whapload Road beneath the cliffs, if only to visit the delightful little maritime museum opposite the Denes or climb the adjacent score to take a closer look at the lighthouse.

This is after all the most easterly point in England, and the coast is littered with dangerous sandbanks. So it is appropriate that the history of Lowestoft High and Low Lights should go back an extraordinarily long way. In 1609 Trinity House responded to petitions from shipowners and merchants to erect two light towers, one on the clifftop and the other on the shingle below, 'for the direction of ships which crept by night in the dangerous passage betwixt Lowestoft and Winterton'. The present High Light (the Low Light no longer exists) dates back to 1676 and was originally coal fired, only protected by a lantern when local people complained about the danger from flying sparks. In 1777 Trinity House experimented with a new form of 'spangle light', a cylinder covered with 4,000 tiny mirrors reflecting a circle of 126 oil lamps. It seems to have worked extremely well, with a luminous range of 20 miles, but it was soon superseded by Argand burners and parabolic reflectors. The powerful modern light is visible for 28 miles, though like all lighthouses, at close quarters it looks deceptively weak. If you could inspect the lantern you would probably find something surprisingly like an outsized domestic light bulb.

Also at this end of the town is a local enterprise, the Raglan Smoke House, that in its own way transcends Lowestoft's fishing history, whether it be trawling for plaice or drifting for herring. Although the street name 'Raglan' indicates a terrace of late 19th century houses, the smoke house almost hidden behind them dates back to 1760, when the harbour did not even exist.

The swing bridge, Oulton.

13

GREAT YARMOUTH AND THE BROADS

> Then up jumped a herring, the queen of the sea,
> Says 'Sorry, old skipper, you'll never catch me'

THE HERRING MAY HAVE been the queen of the sea, as this old Norfolk fishermen's song has it, but the hard fact is that the great fleets of drifters that once crowded Yarmouth's quays were only too efficient at catching it. Overfishing – though not just by the British – destroyed the North Sea stocks that migrated past each autumn.

Since the 1960s fishing has been replaced by offshore gas and oil, followed recently by offshore wind farms – particularly on the Scroby Sands close by – as the main sources of the port's prosperity. The golden weathervane in the form of a steam drifter atop the Town Hall on South

Quay should perhaps be replaced by the equally characteristic shape of an offshore supply vessel, with her piled-up superstructure forward and low working deck aft.

Yarmouth has been adapting to similar changes of fortune over many centuries. Though traces of its early history can certainly be found – sections of the medieval walls, remnants of the narrow fishermen's 'rows' which used to link the river wharves with the open Denes behind the beach, and so on – this is evidently a vigorous community inclined to press on rather than linger in the past.

The former fish wharf now handles a variety of freighters, offshore supply and wind farm support vessels. And although the long-established river port has miles of quayside, described by Defoe even two centuries ago as 'the finest in England, if not in Europe', work began in 2007 on a new deep-water outer harbour beyond the existing entrance, and which opened in 2010. This ambitious project has proved problematic, and locally controversial. But it signals the port's continued determination to play a part in whatever maritime future the North Sea holds.

Yarmouth takes its name from the River Yare which flows through Norwich. But the Yare is also joined at the western end of Breydon Water by the Waveney, diverted north from Lowestoft, and at its eastern end by the Bure which leads upstream into the main Norfolk Broads. In Roman times the shingle spit on which Yarmouth stands was an island in the broad estuary of these three rivers, with a harbour at Caister for ships serving the Rhineland and a fortress at Burgh Castle, the remains of which can still be seen near the confluence of the Waveney and the Yare. By the 14th century, when Yarmouth had developed from a fishing settlement to a major trading port, the northern entrance channel was blocked and a shingle spit was extending across the southern channel; the town began a centuries-long struggle to keep this remaining entrance open.

Each time drifting sand and shingle choked the entrance, money was somehow raised and labour organised to dig a fresh channel somewhere else. Not until 1567, at the seventh attempt, was the present harbour entrance stabilised by wooden piling, under the direction of a Dutch engineer. Yarmouth could now reliably serve and exploit its vast hinterland, including Norwich, through a network of marshy rivers. Wool, worsted and smoked herring were traded for wine, timber and stone.

But it was in the 19th century that the herring in its many forms really took over – pickled in brine for export to Germany and Russia, heavily smoked to become a red herring, split open as a kipper, or lightly smoked as that Yarmouth speciality the bloater. I am told the bloater was only invented in 1836, but ten years later Peggotty in Charles Dickens's *David Copperfield* was already 'proud to call herself a Yarmouth Bloater'.

From the 1850s, when many of the Barking smacks arrived as refugees from the polluted Thames (a maritime migration recorded in the name of the Barking Smack pub on Yarmouth's Marine Parade), a fleet of large ketch-rigged sailing trawlers and drifters rapidly developed. The herring drifters were magnificent vessels, but just as rapidly they were overtaken by steam power, introduced in the 1880s.

Steam drifters were then the latest in technology, yet at this distance in time they have just as much nostalgic charm as their sailing predecessors: straight stems almost leaning back against the pull of the nets, tall funnels and steadying mizzens set above their rounded sterns. Their story, along with many others, is told in Yarmouth's maritime museum, just behind the town quay.

The industry reached its peak in 1913 when well over a thousand vessels worked out of Yarmouth, landing between them 800,000 cran of herring (more than 2 million cwt). Much of this vast catch was gutted and packed into brine-filled barrels on the South Denes by Scots girls who followed the herring's southward North Sea migration each autumn.

The First World War interrupted all this. Drifters were diverted to minesweeping, and though they returned, the industry never fully recovered. Nor for that matter did the herring. The North Sea stocks were overfished and continued their decline after the Second World War. The last Yarmouth drifter was sold in 1963. A year later the first of the drilling rigs began searching for gas off the Norfolk coast.

Yarmouth was superbly placed to serve the new industry, opposite where natural gas was soon found in the southern basin of the North

Yarmouth ... from fish to oil.

Sea, with some quays standing empty, and a small tidal range which allowed the tugs and supply vessels to come and go 24 hours a day. The Norfolk port soon became the main base for the offshore gas industry and second only to Aberbeen as far as oil was concerned. In recent years the offshore wind farms have added their employment, particularly the cluster of turbines easily visible on the nearby Scroby Sands – modern windmills with 130-foot blades each generating two megawatts, commissioned in 2004.

Ashore, the best place to survey all this maritime activity is not in Yarmouth itself but in Gorleston, on the other side of the river entrance, from whose pierhead you can look back along the harbour. Surveying the two communities from this fine vantage point, you get the impression that Gorleston is something of a poor relation, though none the worse for that. This may be the port of Great Yarmouth, but ships negotiating its awkward entrance at night depend for their safety on the guidance of Gorleston's slender red-brick lighthouse (almost precariously slender, in fact, and in need of some repointing when I was last there) to provide a pair of leading lights. The RNLI lifeboat and the harbour pilots are also stationed on this side of the river, with room for

The South Quay at Yarmouth.

one or two small fishing vessels. And in any case Gorleston has its own Edwardian seafront (the splendidly ornate Pavilion Theatre opened in 1901), a wide sandy beach and gardens behind the pier.

Back on the northern side of the river, Yarmouth seafront is the Norfolk coast's answer to Blackpool – a blatant beach resort which first supplanted the longshore salvage companies as it developed in the 19th century, then overwhelmed the elegance of early buildings like the Royal Hotel, which was patronised by both Charles Dickens and Edward VII.

Dickens stayed there in 1847 to write *David Copperfield*. Many of the novel's most important events take place on this beach, including Ham's heroic attempt to rescue Steerforth. Dickens is believed to have modelled Ham on an old sailor called Sharman, the first keeper of the 144ft-high monumental column which stands on the South Denes not far from the harbour entrance. It is known as the Norfolk Pillar, and although the figure on top is Britannia, it was erected in 1819 in honour of Admiral Nelson – into whose navy Sharman had been press-ganged as a boy. During the holiday season you can climb the 217 steps inside and take in the magnificent view.

The Pillar originally stood in the middle of a race course, laid out by the military who garrisoned the Denes during the Napoleonic wars. The barracks were later run by a Captain Manby, a remarkably inventive man who must have seen many vessels in trouble along that difficult shore and devoted a lot of his energy to making things a bit safer for them. He is credited with the idea of giving each lighthouse a characteristic pattern of flashes; he designed Yarmouth's first lifeboat, and he invented a line-throwing mortar with which a breeches buoy could be rigged between a stranded ship and the shore. If Ham had had such a device he might have saved Steerforth, and his own life – but that would have spoilt Dickens's story.

Two and a half miles from Yarmouth's turbulent harbour entrance the lifting Haven Bridge leads into a much quieter world of winding rivers and reed-fringed Broads. But the remarkable fact is that though navigation of the Bure and the Waveney is limited by numerous fixed bridges, until quite recently small seagoing coasters of up to about 500 tons could and did navigate the Yare right into the heart of Norwich – which meant that yachtsmen could follow without lowering their masts, as I have done myself. Even today, Norwich is still technically a port in its own right, though to reach it from the sea 20 miles away a vessel must negotiate three lifting road bridges and two railway swing bridges.

The precedence of boats over motor cars that this implies (something Dutch visitors will take for granted) seems unlikely to survive much longer. The new fixed road east of Norwich has a water clearance of only 35 feet and the Trowse railway swing bridge nearby (its predecessor was the first bridge of this kind in the world) was 'temporarily' welded shut in 2003 and might have remained so, one suspects, had the maritime community not protested.

Many of the specialised sailing boats on the Broads already reckon to lower their masts from time to time, in order to 'quant' through fixed bridges at places like Acle and Potter Heigham. The beautiful old black-sailed trading wherries, Broadland's equivalent of the Thames spritsail barge, did the same. The bottom of their unstayed mast was balanced with about two tons of lead or iron to make the job easier.

The wherries were such shapely craft: mainly clinker built in oak with finely drawn ends, and a single high-peaked gaff sail treated with a black mixture of tar and herring oil. Their downfall was the extreme degree to which they had adapted to their special environment. Apart from the splendid *Albion,* preserved by the Norfolk Wherry Trust, only a few examples have survived.

Seagoing yachtsmen sometimes turn their noses up at the idea of sailing on the Norfolk Broads. Apart from being wrong, they should beware of tangling with a Broads sailor on his or her home waters. These special conditions – never enough room but plenty of wind – breed peculiarly good helmsmen and some of the most elegant and refined sailing boats you will find anywhere. Two to look out for are the White Boat and the Norfolk Punt.

The White Boat is more properly the Yare and Bure One-Design, a pretty three-quarter decked 20-footer with a short bowsprit and gunter rig. The class was founded in 1908 and now number perhaps a hundred boats, spread round the Broads, their white topsides distinguishing them from the varnished Brown Boats. Traditionally they have charming butterfly names like *Clouded Yellow* and *Painted Lady.*

As far as Norfolk is concerned, punt-gunning for wildfowl originated on Breydon Water. The punt itself was a simple, flat-bottomed, slab-sided craft similar to those that developed in Essex and elsewhere, and paddled or occasionally sailed in much the same way. But it was from the rather different Hickling punt, quanted or shoved through the shallow reed beds by a man standing in the stern, that the modern racing boat developed. And whereas in Essex a few gun punts are raced more or less in their original form, here they evolved into a separate and sophisticated boat.

The Hickling technique of shoving the punt along had already encouraged a more complex shape: more beam for stability, flared clinker sides and a slightly rounded carvel bottom. This was the basic hull, 18 to 22 feet long and still relatively cheap to build, that was adopted by sailing enthusiasts between the wars and led to the formation of the Norfolk Punt Club in 1926. Since then the design has grown, in both 'traditional' and modern forms, into one of the most exciting boats you could wish to sail.

14

The Happisburgh Light.

THE NORTH NORFOLK HARBOURS

HAPPISBURGH – CROMER – BLAKENEY – WELLS – BURNHAM OVERY –
BRANCASTER – THORNHAM

THE FIFTY MILES OF Norfolk coastline from Yarmouth to Blakeney is notable not for its harbours but for the lack of them. By sea, the passage does have the advantage that you can carry the tide with you. But Blakeney, for all its charm, is not the most encouraging harbour to reach in a fading light and a strong onshore wind; nor even Wells a few miles farther on, equally exposed though far better buoyed.

The fact is that when the weather is coming from Scandinavia this can be a bleak corner of East Anglia. Not so bad with a powerful diesel engine to comfort you, but to the skippers of the clumsy collier brigs that once used to gather in great fleets to run the gauntlet of the Wash, Cromer bay was known as 'the Devil's throat'. No wonder that Happisburgh's majestic church shelters so many drowned sailors, or that Cromer's famous lifeboat coxswain Henry Blogg should have been awarded more medals than any other.

Travelling north from Yarmouth in the 1720s, Defoe was 'surpris'd to see, in all the way from Winterton, that the farmers, and country people had scarcely a barn, or a shed, or a stable; nay, not the pales of their yards, and gardens, not a hogstye, not a necessary-house, but what was built of old planks, beams, wales and timbers, etc, the wrecks of ships, and ruins of mariners and merchants' fortunes; and in some places were whole yards fill'd, and piled up very high with the same stuff laid up, as I suppos'd to sell for the like building purposes, as there should be occasion'.

Making the same journey today, my recommendation is to ignore the main road in favour of the undulating B1159 that follows the coastline. Beyond Winterton Ness this road skirts the broads at Horsey, meanders through little Sea Palling, crouched behind its marram grass dunes so that from seaward only the church tower reveals its existence, then climbs towards Happisburgh, pronounced Haisboro'. Offshore, when applied to the nearby sands, the name is written as it sounds, but the landsmen's awkward spelling is historically more correct because the settlement or 'burgh' was named after a man called Haep.

To say of Happisburgh that 'you can't miss it' is a heavy understatement. Its great 110 foot church tower was a prominent seamark for three centuries before Trinity House built the nearby lighthouse in 1791. And there had been a smaller church there for centuries before that. The grass mound on the north side of the present building is the mass grave of 119 sailors from HMS *Invincible,* wrecked on the Haisboro' Sand in March 1801. And other graves are marked with anchors. By the end of the 19th century there were so many wrecks along this shore that Trinity House used explosives to clear the beach.

The beginning of the Norfolk fishermen's song I have quoted elsewhere goes like this:

> As we were a fishing off Haisboro' Light,
> Shooting and hauling and trawling all night.
> It was windy old weather, stormy old weather;
> When the wind blows, we all pull together.

In the last verse, after the conger eel has warned that the 'wind's comin' easterly', the song concludes:

> I think what these fishes are saying is right;
> We'll haul up our gear and we'll steer for the Light.

Trinity House originally built two lighthouses here: the red and white banded High Light, which still stands among the clifftop fields, and a Low Light on the beach near the 'cart gap' once used by the small fishing community. This second light used to guide vessels south of the Haisboro' sands but was shut down once a light vessel had been established offshore. The High Light went through the usual progression from candles to Argand burners to automatically controlled electricity, but with one unusual addition: during the 1860s the station experimented with making its own coal gas, accumulated in tanks each day then used to power the lantern at night.

In 1987 Trinity House decided that with the development of electronic navigational aids and the decline in coastal traffic the light was not worth maintaining; fishermen no longer needed it to steer by. This decision roused local people not just to protest but to positive action. An Act of Parliament established the Happisburgh Lighthouse Trust as a 'local light authority' and the great clifftop tower became Britain's only independently operated lighthouse.

Cromer lies not so much on the clifftop as sprawled over it, with a small pier at the bottom of the gap. There you can inspect the two lifeboat houses that Coxswain Henry Blogg knew: the older one on the

Cromer's small fleet of crab boats.

beach; the newer constructed at the pier end in 1923 when the first motor lifeboat arrived. With little shelter in either direction, Cromer's lifeboats have been launched many hundreds of times since the station was first established in the early 19th century, saving well over a thousand lives.

At the bottom of the cliff gap, Cromer's small fleet of crab boats, about a dozen of them, work from the beach with their attendant launching tractors. They used to be wooden craft, boldly painted in traditional red, white and blue, whose simple, double-ended design went back almost directly to the Middle Ages and perhaps beyond that to the Vikings. Before the days of tractors they would be carried across the flats slung from oars slotted through their gunwhales. Only one of the traditional boats was still working when I last called by; the rest have given way to fast outboard-powered fibreglass designs – which still do the same job in the same exacting conditions.

Cromer is a hydrographic turning point. From here the Norfolk coast runs almost due west for about 40 miles. From Blakeney onwards its protecting banks are pierced every few miles – at Wells, Burnham Overy, Brancaster and little Thornham – by narrow half-tide channels that wind into small quays or staithes. And whereas the sand and shingle spits extending across such entrances as the Yare, the Ore and the Deben tend to grow southwards, here they stretch westwards.

Blakeney shelters behind such a spit, whose growth can be traced in successive 'casts' of shingle marking former entrances. Owned by the National Trust, it was established in the early years of this century as one of Britain's first nature reserves. The old lifeboat house stands near the end and a former Coastguard watch house halfway along.

The quay at Blakeney.

The flood tide sluices round the point to fill the sandy channel to the town quay suddenly and violently for just an hour or two at high water. The launches which take holidaymakers out to view the seals suffer in extreme form from the frustration that afflicts anyone who goes boating from the head of a tidal waterway: they struggle out against the tide as soon as it makes and then struggle back against it before the water disappears. Once it does one can walk, mostly on clean sand, where minutes before boats were chugging past. You may see the bait diggers striding off, forks over their shoulders. Digging up lugworms – irresistible to fish – has been quite an industry on this stretch of coast. They are bought and sold by the hundred, counted out like sweets. Peter Brooks's town guide recalls that a champion worm digger called Ellis 'Mutton' Bishop could bag 11,000 of the creatures in a day.

Blakeney today is a smart little holiday and sailing resort, equipped with the appropriate hotels, pubs and craft shops. But this modern growth has been grafted onto an ancient and at times quite prosperous small port. Hence the monumental parish church with its extra beacon tower on the northeast corner, and the elaborately brick-vaulted undercroft of the ruined 15th century Guildhall, or the Mariners' Hill next to it on the quayside. This mound is believed to be man-made, either as a fortification or simply to allow merchants to check and signal to vessels anchored in the deep-water 'Pit' inside Blakeney Point – well worth a short climb for the view.

Photographs taken at the turn of the century show several trading ketches moored at the quay, even a tiny steam tug. But for a long time then the harbour had gradually been silting up, largely due to the damming of neighbouring creeks at Salthouse and Cley (now a birdwatchers' Mecca run by the Norfolk Wildlife Trust, with a convenient car park). And the railway never came to encourage a fresh start. Sometime between the wars, Blakeney stopped being a port and became a holiday resort.

Wells-next-the-Sea also earns part of its living as a holiday town. But unlike its neighbour, it can point proudly to a continued existence as a commercial port. The cargo vessels that used to serve the quayside silo have admittedly gone, but a number of fishing vessels are still based there. They set pots for whelks, crabs and lobsters as the creatures migrate and mingle amongst the offshore sands (the pots differ, but all are designed to make entering easy and escaping difficult). Most ambitiously, a completely new outer harbour has been carved out of the shingle for catamarans servicing the Sheringham Shoal wind farm, which began generating in 2011.

The harbour's curious shape comes from the fact that in the middle of the last century a mile-long dyke was built down the centre of what was formerly a symmetrical network of marshy channels sheltering behind Bob Hall's Sand. Those to the east remain; to the west they have been drained and reclaimed, including the creek which made Holkham an active Elizabethan port.

Entering Wells by road along the A149 from Blakeney, you skirt the edge of Church Marsh where the medieval harbour reached round the back of the town, a topography temporarily reasserted by the 1953 floods. Turn left on to the main quay and you have reached the maritime heart of the town. Here the man-made approach channel known as 'The Run' turns through a right angle past the harbour office and pontoons, the fishery berths and the former silo – now converted into spectacular flats.

The Norfolk whelk fishery developed at Sheringham in the late 1800s, initially for bait and then to satisfy London's vast appetite for boiled shellfish. For some time, however, Wells seems to have been its most important centre. I can remember how reassuring it was to meet the homecoming fleet off their intimidating harbour entrance when I first visited Wells in the 1950s. The boats sometimes motor more than 30 miles offshore and back to lay their cylindrical baited pots in deep water. The whelks climb in through the top, attracted by a whiff of salted fish, but cannot manage the return trip.

To appreciate the dramatic nature of the Wells harbour entrance, you should drive out behind the bank that protects fields and caravans to the west of the harbour and inspect the channel, preferably at low tide, from the shingle point where the lifeboat house stands. The bar is still

The RNLI Lifeboat Station at Wells.

1½ miles away across the flat sands. At high tide the winding channel is well marked by pairs of red and green buoys. As the tide recedes there is no need for navigation marks; what is left of the channel is only too obvious. Half the buoys end up canted against the shingle.

Breaking seas on the bar did their worst on 29 October, 1880 when the lifeboat capsized trying to make harbour. Eleven of the thirteen crew members were drowned, leaving ten widows with 27 children in the town.

In those days the lifeboat house was at the west end of the main quay, which meant her crew had to pull 2½ miles to reach open water, often against wind and tide. The present house was accordingly built farther out, launching into the adjacent channel, or wherever the nearest sufficiently deep water can be found.

The Wells boat must be the only lifeboat anyone has ever tried to steal. Seven German prisoners-of-war tried it one night, impatient to get home at the end of the Second World War, but they could not start the engine.

Leaving Wells on the A129, heading westward, you pass Holkham Hall, once the estate of 'Coke of Norfolk' and now open to the public. Though its creek may long ago have been sacrificed in the interests of agriculture, the lane leading down to Holkham Gap on the right opens onto a superb nautical amphitheatre which offers perfect sheltered bathing at high tide and fine walking along the dunes.

From there the road passes a succession of small harbours tucked in behind the dunes, each with its own staithe or quay. The easternmost is Burnham Overy Staithe, one of the 'seven Burnhams'.

This is Nelson's country, so much so that he is referred to on the pub sign simply as 'The Hero'. His father was the rector at Burnham Thorpe. Almost any stretch of water round here is reputed to be 'where Nelson learned to sail', though Brancaster probably has the best claim as his childhood nurse married the landlord of The Ship inn there. He certainly knew Burnham Overy Staithe well. The Nelsonian biographer Tom Pocock quotes a letter to Fanny Nelson in which he boasted that his new command, the *Agamemnon,* had become 'as well known through Europe as one of Mr Harwood's boats is at Overy'. It's said that while he was an unemployed captain 'on the beach', he would walk the sea walls pondering the news from France and whether the Navy might need him again.

Overy Staithe ... perhaps the prettiest of the North Norfolk harbours.

These days the local sailing tends to be done in smart little varnished dinghies and yellow wellies; but it's none the worse for that. The popular sea wall walks, looping out to seaward from the roadside villages, are often sign-posted by the various organisations caring for these salt marsh and sand dune habitats under the umbrella of the Norfolk Heritage Coast. The walls also form an extension of the Peddars Way, the Roman road which begins at Castle Acre.

Scolt Head, the hump like a basking seal on the northern horizon when you look out from Brancaster Staithe, is owned by the National Trust and managed as a reserve by the Norfolk Wildlife Trust. Scolt becomes an island at high tide, sheltering Overy Staithe under its eastern arm and Brancaster Staithe to the west.

Overy Staithe is perhaps the prettiest of these small North Norfolk harbours, probably developed there as silting and reclamation combined to prevent ships working up the river to Burnham Overy itself. However, Brancaster Staithe, with its derelict brick quay and cluster of mussel fishermen's huts (Brancaster mussels are much prized and much advertised in the smart local restaurants), is somewhat easier to visualise as what it once was, a substantial medieval port.

Looking at Scolt Head from Brancaster.

In fact its history goes back way beyond that. The name evidently derives from the Roman fortress of Branodunum, the northernmost of a chain of similar forts built to defend the 'Saxon shore' against North Sea raiders. Others were at Burgh Castle, behind Yarmouth, possibly at Dunwich, at Walton-next-Felixstowe – somewhere submerged off Harwich – and at Bradwell in Essex. The site of the 3rd century fort is about a mile away from the staithe, on the seaward side of the A149 just as you run into Brancaster.

If you have time before leaving Brancaster Staithe take a look at the little round-towered church at the eastern end of the village, which really belongs to Burnham Deepdale. Round towers are typical of this area; this one is Saxon, supposedly made that shape because the absence of corners enabled the builders to work with a crude mixture of flint and 'puddingstone'. The little church has medieval stained glass and a remarkable Norman font that shows the months of the year from a farm labourer's point of view: digging in March, weeding in June, harvesting in August, grinding the corn in October, killing a pig in November and communal feasting in December.

Thornham is the last and smallest of this group of harbours, what in Essex we would call a gutway. Yet this too came into its own as a port in the 16th century. I gather there was a coal store here, and granaries, the last of them swept away by the 1953 floods. All that is left now is a strange, indecipherable group of twisted tree stumps, clearly once planted by man but looking more like the remains of a petrified forest.

Thornham ... like the remains of a petrified forest.

15

The cliffs at Hunstanton.

KING'S LYNN

IT IS A WONDER to me that King's Lynn has not long since been swept out into the Wash, along with King John's jewels. After studying with some astonishment the successive flood levels marked on the west doorway of St Margaret's Church, and then walking over to the river bank to watch the Great Ouse sluicing past, I find it difficult to understand how any town could withstand such a combination.

In 1953 the town's sea defences were overwhelmed with devastating swiftness. According to contemporary accounts, a train on its way from Hunstanton simply ran into a wall of water, and having stood its ground was struck by a wooden bungalow floating past. Yet the record marked in stone at St Margaret's shows that in 1978 the flood water rose even higher!

Floods must always have been a hazard in this fenland town, but the Great Ouse was not always the fiercely concentrated stream it is today. Having become a great medieval port serving northern Europe – even adopted by the Hanseatic League, one of whose warehouses can still be seen – Lynn joined other East Coast harbours fighting to keep the silt at bay and if possible create deeper channels for bigger ships. One approach was to drain the fens more directly, which helped a good deal. Another plan, eventually carried through in the 19th century, was to straighten the sweeping S-bend on which the town had stood. Again it was an improvement, but this was still very much a tidal port and the final stage of 19th century development was to dig two wet docks, the Alexandra and the Bentinck, and link them to an expanding railway system.

King's Lynn is now a busy, thoroughly modern port equipped to handle a whole variety of cargoes – aggregates, grain, timber, fertilisers, metals, petroleum products – with a focus on the requirements of the local farming industry. Vessels of up to 5,000 tons can now turn south

The Bank House in King's Lynn.

at the Roaring Middle light float and use the short, powerful flood tide to reach the dock gates before the Great Ouse reasserts itself. It takes about an hour and a half for the flood stream to get going in the river, but once it does the level swiftly rises, by more than 20 feet on spring tides. Turning such big vessels when they arrive requires masterly precision.

The town was named King's Lynn by Henry VIII, but it is still often referred to simply as Lynn. A community of this substance did not need many favours, even from the king. Defoe, as usual, was quick to identify the geographical basis of its early trading success. 'The reason whereof is this', he wrote in his 18th century *Tour*, 'that there are more navigable rivers empty themselves here into the sea, including the Washes which are branches of the same port, than at any one mouth of waters in England, except the Thames and the Humber. By these navigable rivers the merchants of Lynn supply about six counties wholly, and three counties in part, with their goods, especially wine and coals.' Baltic timber was another major import, and the export of wool had played its part as it did elsewhere in East Anglia.

Fortunately, the wealth this trade created was invested in an extraordinary succession of fine buildings we can still enjoy. The people of Lynn seem to have had a special flair for architecture; they even elected an architect as mayor. John Betjeman once described the waterfront route along Nelson, Queen and King Streets as 'the finest walk in Europe', and many of the buildings he admired are connected with the sea.

At the southern end, the former Greenland Fishery was once the local pub for the men who serviced the whaling ships berthed in the River Nar's deep little gutway nearby. In St Margaret's Lane, off Nelson Street, you can see the 15th century Hanseatic warehouses which handled cargoes from the North German ports until 1750. Clifton House on Queen Street has a five-storeyed watchtower in its walled garden. Just beyond that, alongside one of the 'fleets' which originally divided Lynn into three islands, is the Customs House, designed by Mayor Henry Bell in the Palladian style. And since a harbour like this lives and works by the tides, St Margaret's Church has a beautiful 17th century moon clock which tells the time of high water. The church, incidentally, is an extraordinary collage of different styles and periods, including some clustered columns that have drifted alarmingly over the years – a style known locally, so Chris Springham told me, as 'slarntndicular'. The towers flanking the west door do not match, because when the foundations gave way under the northerly one in 1452 the townspeople decided to rebuild it in what was then the smart new Perpendicular style. The difference between the towers was accentuated by the addition of a tall spire to the southern one. But in the great storm of 8 September, 1741 that fell down, wrecking the nave, which was rebuilt in yet another style.

At the other end of the town Chris and I came across another architectural curiosity – in the bar of the old established Ouse Amateur Sailing Club. Since this was Lynn, the disastrous 1953 flood level was recorded on the wall. But members proudly pointed out that the bar's rubber sealed glass doors were part of the official sea defences. At the next flood warning, the consumption of real ale could continue uninterrupted.

When the club was founded in 1881, the word 'amateur' presumably meant that members did their own sailing, without relying on the paid

The Great Ouse, King's Lynn.

help of local boatmen. However, anyone sailing out of Lynn needs to be thoroughly professional in the modern sense of the word, if only to cope with that ferocious flood tide, running at up to seven knots. In fact at the time of writing there were no large sailing yachts based there, although the harbour authorities were planning in 2013 to install a pontoon at the quay so that visiting yachts might lie afloat.

At the northern end of the town, where a name like Pilot Street recalls that this was once the fishing quarter, is the Tuesday Market Place (there is also a Saturday Market Place at the southern end). A friendly enough place these days, but with a grim history. The town gallows and pillory were once here, and in 1590 a 'witch finder' singled out the wretched Margaret Read to be burnt alive. It is said that her heart burst out through the flames, struck a nearby house and then jumped into the River Ouse. The black mark it left (a heart shape enclosed in a diamond) is recorded above the blind white doorway of the red brick offices on the northern side of the square.

Lynn's 'Fisher Fleet' or creek used to run through this corner of the town until the 19th century docks blocked its upper end. There has long been an active fishing community here which once ranged as far as Iceland in search of cod for salting and now supplies an international market with shrimps, mussels and cockles.

To reach the modern Fleet, take the northwward road skirting the docks (the A1078) and turn down Cross Bank Road. You will find a narrow, muddy inlet packed with an unusual variety of boats, some obviously built a long way from Norfolk: a few old wooden smacks or bawleys, and plenty of the brutally powered, square-sterned steel craft that are their modern equivalents – just the place for anyone who likes looking at boats and their gear. The heavy, wire-meshed dredges are for mussels, the nets for shrimps, and the heavy rusting pipework for dredging cockles.

One reason for arbitrarily beginning this guide at Leigh and ending it at Lynn is the natural symmetry between the sandbanks which funnel shipping into the Thames and those which almost choke this southeast corner of the Wash – names like Thief, Seal, Blackguard and Bull Dog.

And similar conditions create similar fisheries, including cockling; the fishing methods, and sometimes the vessels themselves, move from one port to another in the constant search for a catch.

The only time I went cockling from Lynn it was with a semi-retired fisherman and his son who used the traditional raking method – dropping anchor on a likely bank he had previously marked, 'blowing' the cockles into a heap with his propeller by swinging against the receding tide, then jumping on to the drying sand to begin raking into sacks.

At the time it seemed unlikely that this laborious old method would last in competition with modern dredging. Water-pumped dredges – originally a Dutch idea, apparently – had been tried out on the Thames at Leigh in the 1960s and rapidly took over. The new technology spread north to the Wash, yet now I'm told, because of the damage caused by uncontrolled dredging, raking is once more in fashion. If he's still around, my old skipper will be delighted.

ACKNOWLEDGEMENTS AND REFERENCES

Most of the original research for this guide consisted of revisiting places to check my memory of facts, topography, routes and pubs; bringing myself up to date on harbour works, shipping traffic or fishing as I did so. In some instances, where Chris Springham knew a place better than I did, he did a lot more than provide the illustrations.

Research of this pleasurable kind – now substantially repeated for this new edition – involves asking innumerable questions of strangers you meet along the way, so my main thanks go to the many who took trouble to give me a courteous answer – fishermen, harbour masters, historians, lifeboatmen, yacht club secretaries, clergymen (particularly the Rector of Brightlingsea church, who turned out to tell me the story of the tiles), and Trinity House pilots.

Among those I can thank individually are first of all my wife Pamela, who showed her invariable patience and supportiveness. My brother John put me right about Manningtree, Mistley and the Stour. Chris Bailey did the same at Leigh. The musician Dr W. H. Swinburne gave me the flavour of old Lowestoft. At Wells I received a lot of help and information from local sailor Peter Rainsford and lifeboat coxswain Allen Frary. In my home town of Maldon, I benefited from the late Mike Townsend's deep knowledge of wildfowling, and the Osborne family took great trouble in showing me round their salt works.

One of the pleasures of writing this book has been having an excuse not only to revisit old haunts along the East Anglian coast but also to read again old favourites from my bookshelf, such as Hervey Benham's *Once Upon a Tide* and *Down Tops'l*. I am glad to acknowledge my debt to him. Also to John Leather – for if I were ever inclined to imagine I knew everything about my own adopted river, the Blackwater, his book *The Salty Shore* would be there to prove me wrong. If it is boats that brought you to the East coast, these are among the first you should turn to for further information.

An obvious point of comparison for my own discursive sort of guide is Archie White's *Tideways and Byways of Essex and Suffolk*, still happily available though it was written not long after the Second World War. Probably less well known is Wilfrid Wren's *Ports of the Eastern Counties*, which I commend to anyone who wants to follow up historical references to the development of the major commercial ports along this coast. Another Terence Dalton book I gave myself for Christmas some years ago is Gordon Kinsey's *Bawdsey, Birth of the Beam*, which tells in every detail how those great radar masts came to be built at the entrance to the River Deben.

While working through my own county I always had Reaney's *The Place-names of Essex* handy, along with Hilda Grieve's great work on

the 1953 floods. If in doubt about a point of architecture, I turned to Pevsner's *The Buildings of England* for adjudication.

Among the local guides I can particularly recommend are Jean and Stuart Bacon's historical booklets, especially the one on Dunwich, where they have done a great deal of research on the lost city. Also Carol and Michael Weaver's history of Woodbridge, the 'Poppyland' series covering Yarmouth and Blakeney, and Alan Bottomley and Joan Hutchinson's beautifully produced *Discovering Southwold*.

I make no apology for quoting chunks of Defoe, whose 18th century *Tour* is still a surprisingly valuable background for someone travelling the East Anglian coast, nor for reminding readers of the sheer passion to be found in *Mehalah* and *The History of Margaret Catchpole*. Both novels were written by 19th century clergymen and have been republished by the Boydell Press. They evoke the Essex and Suffolk coasts as *Wuthering Heights* does the Yorkshire moors. Crabbe's poetry does the same for Aldeburgh, where I had expert local guidance from my sister Trixie.

INDEX